What People Are Saying...

"Anyone with an interest in launching a startup should read this book and will be glad they did."

> — **William H. Draper III, Venture Capitalist, Author of *The Startup Game* and Co-Chair of the Draper Richards Kaplan Foundation**

"Hou breaks down many of the daunting tasks facing a founder into actionable steps. Chock full of tips, *Startups Demystified* is like having a mentor walk you through the collective wisdom of how other founders have successfully passed through the same stages."

> — **Ravi Belani, Managing Director, Alchemist Accelerator and Lecturer of Entrepreneurship at Stanford University**

"Practical and actionable advice that entrepreneurs of all kinds can use."

> — **Kerry Healey, President, Babson College and former Lieutenant Governor of Massachusetts**

"Hou has taken the perspectives of new and aspiring founders and addressed their needs head on. Technological improvements have magnified the opportunities for young persons to create a wide variety of new platforms, products, and services that serve important social needs. At MIT Sloan, we encourage wholeheartedly our students to become responsible global citizens with the vision, drive, and real-world experience to contribute and generate new solutions to existing challenges. This guide unveils the startup process so enterprising young people can turn their worthwhile ideas into reality."

> — **David C. Schmittlein, Dean, MIT Sloan School of Management**

"In this highly readable handbook, Barbara Hou provides an invaluable checklist for the budding entrepreneur. Drawing on personal experience as an entrepreneur, and on her avid interest on the subject, Barbara has distilled the key questions that those who want to create a venture must answer. For those with urgency to change the world this book distills the wisdom they need to be planful in 75 simple lessons. A great read!"

— **Fernando M. Reimers, Professor, Harvard University**

"Barbara highlights how exciting it is for my generation to watch millennials come up with innovative ideas and new ways of doing things. No longer constrained by traditional employment, entrepreneurship provides this forward-thinking generation with a realistic career option. This book helps makes that option even more possible."

— **Diane Propsner, Huffington Post**

"An indispensable companion whether you are a for-profit, nonprofit, or social entrepreneur. We need entrepreneurs to make use of the ideas in here so society can benefit from their important and creative efforts. This book could not have come at a more propitious time."

— **Tom Kosnik, Lecturer, Stanford University and Coauthor of** *Gear Up: Test Your Business Model Potential and Plan your Path to Success*

"As someone who was personally involved in a start-up college designed and delivered by a start-up educational consulting company, I can attest to the many useful tips in this book. I recommend that all entrepreneurs read this book if they are going to do a start-up venture."

— **Shahid Ansari, Professor, Babson College and CEO, Babson Global**

"A motivating story of how a bright idea can turn into a startup business."

— **Letty Calvo, Entrepreneur (Founder and CEO, Vera Mona)**

"A no-nonsense book that describes how the entrepreneurial process works on the day-to-day level. This will minimize surprises and prepare new innovators to take the next critical steps."

— **Wingee Sin, Managing Director, State Street Global Advisors, and Coauthor of** *Impact With Wings: Stories to Inspire and Mobilize Women Angel Investors and Entrepreneurs*

STARTUPS DEMYSTIFIED

Founders Share Strategies, Secrets, and Lessons Learned

BARBARA HOU

First Edition By

CoffeeCupPress

First Published in the United States by
CoffeeCupPress, LLC.
New York, NY, U.S.A.
www.coffeecuppressLLC.com

As of press time, the URLs displayed in this book link or refer to existing websites on the Internet. CoffeeCupPress, LLC is not responsible for, and should not be deemed to endorse or recommend, any website other than its own or any content available on the Internet (including without limitation any website, blog page, or information page) that is not created by CoffeeCupPress. In addition, this publication is sold with the understanding that the publisher is not engaged in rendering legal, financial, or other professional services. If you require legal or financial advice or other expert assistance, you should seek the services of a competent professional.

Library of Congress Cataloging-in-Publication Data

    Hou, Barbara, author.
      Startups demystified : founders share strategies,
    secrets, and lessons learned / Barbara Hou. -- First
    edition.
      pages cm
      Includes bibliographical references and index.
      LCCN 2016911532
      ISBN 978-0692822951

      1. New business enterprises. 2. Organizational
    effectiveness. 3. Entrepreneurship. I. Title.

    HD62.5.H6828 2016   658.1'1
                      QBI16-900030

Printed in the United States of America
10 9 8 7 6 5 4 3 2 1
First Edition

This book is dedicated to my mother, Sharon Hou,
the most entrepreneurial person I know.

Acknowledgements

Many thanks to all the people who helped me with this book. First, to Sue Wang for inspiring and encouraging me to write it. Sometimes you don't know you're capable of something until someone tells you you are. Second, to the friends who connected with many of the founders that I spoke to, including Liz Kwo and Kevin Stone. Without their leads, I wouldn't have met such diverse and enterprising founders. Third, to the individuals who helped me through the editing and revising stages of the book, in particular: Jason Towne, Harlan Edelman, Aaron Adair, Ezra Feldman, Jocelyn Mosman and Carolyn Hou. Their helpful suggestions greatly enhanced the final product. A great many others provided comments, feedback, and reactions to the draft, assistance for which was invaluable. Fourth, to the students in my entrepreneurship classes at Harvard University who responded so positively to the lessons contained in these pages.

Finally, to all the founders who participated in the interviews. They are too many to name here but, without their stories, I wouldn't have been able to capture the lessons and strategies that demystify the entrepreneurial process. I am grateful for the insight they provided and to have met such impressive persons who inspire me, who will inspire others, and who I have no doubt will continue to succeed on their entrepreneurial paths.

Table of Contents

Expanded Table of Contents

Foreword

I have spent over 50 years working with entrepreneurs in Silicon Valley. At the heart of my interest has been a desire to support innovation and entrepreneurial advancement at all levels. I am delighted that this compendium of advice from current entrepreneurs to new and aspiring ones paves the way for more innovative and worthwhile ideas to come to fruition. This is a book written for those who may be on unsure footing and aren't sure how to accomplish what they want to accomplish, but know that they must try. Anyone who wants to transform a worthy creative idea into reality must read this book.

Through her interviews and based on her own experience founding a startup, Barbara Hou describes the strategies and processes that all entrepreneurs need. The reader will learn that entrepreneurship is about more than having a compelling idea. It's equally about leadership skills that are essential to an organization's success. In addition to leadership, successful entrepreneurs must have endurance, initiative, and follow-through.

At the Draper Richards Kaplan Foundation, where we provide grants and support to social entrepreneurs, we ask ourselves, "*Can this entrepreneur handle challenges? Manage people? Communicate effectively? Strategically access opportunities?*" To be a successful entrepreneur one will need to demonstrate a full spectrum of competencies. This book shares specific ways to do so. It also emphasizes the entrepreneur's responsibility to retain high ethical standards and emotional maturity at a time when his or her moral center is tested as never before.

If you read this book, you will learn to tell your "public narrative" about why and how you became committed to a compelling startup idea or cause. You will learn specific phrases to help you more easily garner early assistance. It will teach you how to move from idea to launch, how to recruit and manage a board, and how to make your first sale. You'll also learn that your responsibility as the leader of your enterprise is to discover processes that can be applied at scale. These are examples of the varied types of skills and competencies you'll need to quickly learn within the first few years of startup life. Rather than blindly experiencing these lessons, this guide prepares you to anticipate them.

This book peels back the curtain on young, struggling entrepreneurs and shares specific, practical advice that they can immediately use. Each tip highlights that entrepreneurship is not something magical, but a series of small, discrete steps and practices.

The book is significant because it can help young entrepreneurs to succeed. Across many college campuses today, in the US and abroad, entrepreneurship is becoming a new form of learning experience. My own son Tim recently launched the annual Draper Competition for Collegiate Women Entrepreneurs organized by Smith College. Draper University, also his creation, offers a startup boot camp and crash course in business innovation and entrepreneurship.

This book is another way to pass on the baton of knowledge about startups and entrepreneurial tips to the next generation.

William H. Draper III
Venture Capitalist, Author of *The Startup Game*, and Co-Chair of the Draper Richards Kaplan Foundation
Atherton, California

Preface

During a Christmas Eve sleepover a few years ago, my friend Sue Wang and I stayed up very late and reflected on the events of the past year. We talked, especially, about our efforts to launch new enterprises: Sue had founded her own law firm, Clarity Law Group, while I had founded an educational startup with the admittedly ambitious goal of establishing a global leadership university that would serve women from Asia and the Middle East.

I had first conceived of the Asian Women's Leadership University Project in 2010 and had been working towards its realization for four years – dedicating some portion of every day (and many sleepless nights) to figuring out how to cultivate the support of critical individuals who might advance the goal of creating a new university. Whenever I speak at conferences, and especially when I am around young people, I am asked how I came up with and moved forward with this rather daunting idea, especially as someone neither particularly well-connected, nor wealthy, nor established.

The vision was to establish a vibrant academic institution that would attract students from the Middle East, South Asia, Southeast Asia, and East Asia. It would be a small university modeled on the US Seven Sisters liberal arts colleges (and especially my own alma mater, Smith College). This private, nonprofit institution would tentatively be called the Asian Women's Leadership University (AWLU). I hoped it would become a beacon of opportunity for women, a center of academic excellence, and a convening ground for all those who believed in the full participation of women in society.

The AWLU would be an academically elite institution and would offer a first rate liberal arts education – where even its American supporters might send their own daughters. But it would not be a university only for the privileged. The university would initiate programs to spot and nurture talent, would offer scholarships to promising students, and would greatly enhance and expand opportunities for girls' education in the region. AWLU would thus support the growth of human potential. The university would also welcome fee-paying students from more advantaged backgrounds, especially if they could demonstrate high academic potential, a commitment to social justice, and a desire to use their education for the advancement of their communities, their countries, and their professions.

AWLU would be a bricks-and-mortar institution. Even as MOOCs (massive open online courses) were beginning to transform the face of higher education worldwide, I wanted AWLU to have a physical presence where students from different cultures would live and grow together, learn from each other's experiences, and exchange ideas in person. I saw value in the close interactions of a diverse group of students, young women who came from different linguistic, national, religious, ethnic, and socioeconomic backgrounds. I believed that daily interactions and cultural co-mingling on a lively residential campus would foster the kind of growth and learning that would most benefit students.

With this ambitious vision in mind, I set out in the summer of 2010 on a quest to bring it to life. How naïve! How audacious! How implausible! All probably true. Nonetheless, I started working on this idea and recruited a team. Slowly, but surely. Step by step. And within several months there was significant progress. We drafted an initial concept paper, developed a website and a system to collect online donations, and engaged an international law firm to help us incorporate as a US nonprofit organization with charitable status. We recruited a board of directors, an international advisory council, a global set of supporters, and prominent local champions from the host country, Malaysia. We engaged Smith College as a chief academic planning partner and Perdana-Johns Hopkins Medical School (Malaysia) as a graduate pathway partner. We obtained recognition from the Malaysian Prime Minister as an "Entry Point Project" that would help catalyze Malaysia's national development and its transformation to a knowledge-based economy.

We also managed to identify 100 acres of land in Penang State for a potential campus, and we obtained the personal support of the Chief Minister of Penang. We developed a communications platform with online presence through Facebook and Twitter. We received media attention in publications such as the New York Times, the Huffington Post, and GOOD Magazine, as well as speaking opportunities including the TEDx forums. We raised initial seed funding of US$100,000 from 100 "inaugural founding sponsors" who were friends and family of those associated with the project. These funds paid for web hosting fees, flights for donor or board cultivation meetings, and other costs. We then started securing five and six figure gifts. By the end of 2013, we obtained our first seven-figure gift, bringing our total donations to US$6.13 million. This was not a bad feat given that we were raising funds based purely on an idea! It was incredibly moving to share our vision and to find that people believed in the idea and in us.

By the end of 2014, we had submitted the final elements required by Malaysia's Ministry of Education: commitments of 20 million Malaysian Ringgit (at the time equaling approximately US$6 million) towards the project and a full licensing application, a 100+ page document that detailed the vision, plans, and strategies for launching the AWLU. We had achieved all of this through the ongoing effort of devoted volunteers united by a common purpose and a dedicated international dialing line! But alas, at the final hour, the Malaysian government denied the application for a license to establish the university. By that point, our team, myself included, were too burnt out to focus on finding another host country. Thus, despite the tremendous hope we had for the project and the good progress we had made, our startup came to a close.

During that late Christmas Eve conversation, Sue and I reflected on our respective experiences in founding our own enterprises, on the challenges we faced in doing so, and on what we had learned from these challenges. As I rattled off nonchalantly some of what I had learned through the process of founding and leading the AWLU Project, Sue arose abruptly from the couch. For someone who is often described as sloth-like for her slow, wispy movements, she seemed to have leapt off the couch and bolted to her bedroom, only to return instantly with a notebook and pen.

By candlelight, Sue started scribbling down some of the main points I had mentioned moments earlier. She asked me to repeat some of the thoughts I had shared on leadership, networking, motivation, decision-making, and team dynamics. She was taking notes, her eyes cast down on her yellow legal notepad and her wrist in motion. Then, as she lifted her eyes from the paper, she commented that I should write a book about the lessons learned and insights gained while working on the AWLU Project. I was astounded. I didn't think I had anything of value to share. But if Sue – my brilliant and talented friend – thought I did, then perhaps I did. This was the first moment when I, and perhaps when we both, realized that there might be something worth sharing with others here. Sue, an accomplished lawyer and author herself, persuaded me to dive into the writing of this book, and to share as honestly and as best as I could how I navigated the unwieldy but inspiring AWLU Project.

Those four years were an incredible personal and professional journey for me. This book memorializes the lessons learned from that experience and exhorts new and aspiring founders to pursue their big dreams. I hope that the insights shared here will inspire other people, especially young people, to conceive bold ideas and to pursue them with courage and optimism. I also want to explain that there are in fact methods and even tricks to this process, and that entrepreneurship and leadership are achieved through specific steps that anyone can take and that will bring noticeable results in the pursuit of one's goals. I hope that in writing this book, I can make others and especially young people more able to succeed at launching their innovative and deeply worthwhile ventures.

Thank you for picking this up and leafing through it. I hope you will find some valuable morsels for you and your venture. And thanks to Sue for believing that this was worth writing.

Introduction

This is a book for aspiring founders, entrepreneurs, and activists who are seeking strategies to move their startup ideas to fruition. College and graduate students, and young professionals, increasingly form a **generation of young founders** whom I am calling "Generation F". More than ever, young people are sidestepping traditional career tracks at least for a while to try their hand at the world of entrepreneurship.

Members of Generation F have been influenced by the success stories of Facebook, Airbnb, Twitter, and other companies. They have witnessed the birth of smartphones, and the plethora of apps and the startups behind them, crowd funding platforms, coding academies, and the rise of social entrepreneurship. Their disenchantment with corporate America has combined with an optimism about authoring their own futures. Their youthful eagerness has been propelled by the spread of entrepreneurship courses, school sponsored-hackathons, university-hosted 3-day startup programs, accelerator programs, even Thiel Fellowships, and the creation of "innovation labs." These developments underscore the recent excitement about entrepreneurship on university campuses across the US.

You may be part of Generation F and contemplating, or you may already have begun, launching a startup. If you feel unsure about how to start a startup, or if you are hoping to find a mentor to guide you through the uncertainties and challenges that will litter your entrepreneurial journey, this book was written for you.

As a young entrepreneur myself, trying to establish a global leadership university dedicated to women from Asia and the Middle East, I experienced my own set of successes, mistakes, and failures. From start to finish, I was navigating an arena of crushing uncertainties, constantly in need of a North Star. Was I onto a good idea or was this foolish thinking? Did I have my priorities straight, pursuing the best strategies? Did I have the right people working with me? Was I using resources and tapping connections as effectively as possible? What else was I missing? I desperately wanted to find a mentor to guide me through the launch and leadership of my startup. As it turned out, I never did find mentorship in one single person; instead I found it in a collection of individuals: friends, family, board members, advisors, classmates, sympathetic supporters, and even taxi drivers. With help from innumerable conversations and serendipitous encounters, I managed my startup journey one step at a time.

My experiences as a young founder mirrored the experiences of many other new founders: we flitted from one conversation or encounter to another, collecting piecemeal bits of advice and scattered scraps of wisdom as we fumbled along. We felt our way through the dark, trying to discern the secret path to startup traction, support, and success.

This blind journey, however, can be illuminated. It turns out that entrepreneurs utilize a relatively predictable set of **processes and mindsets** to catalyze their startup ventures. This book captures the common themes and lessons that many founders that I talked with obtained from the process of launching their startups. It distills wisdom often passed down word-of-mouth into a comprehensive and yet specific text.

Within these pages you will find a map to the entrepreneurial landscape, drawn from my interviews with over seventy founders, many of them in their third or fourth year of entrepreneurship. At this stage, founders have gained some entrepreneurial wisdom and have some valuable lessons to impart. Yet they are not so far along as to have forgotten the daunting struggles of the earliest days of launching their ventures. These founders confided their mistakes, shared important lessons learned, and articulated effective strategies that you can apply to your own startup. This book also draws upon my own experiences of founding and leading a startup (and raising US$6 million in the process).

While there is certainly no shortage of books about entrepreneurial strategy, many of them do not focus on the day-to-day tactical challenges that young entrepreneurs face. This book, by contrast, takes on the **perspectives of young founders** and focuses precisely on challenges and concerns that are overlooked by texts written by wildly successful entrepreneurs who have forgotten what it means to start something when you're young, not wealthy, not established, and not particularly well-connected.

To capture the most universal principles, I interviewed founders in a range of industries, including healthcare, medical devices, retail software, education technology, professional services, solar energy, community nonprofits, consumer analytics, automated machinery, food products, and crowdsourcing. I also spoke with founders from a variety of racial, ethnic, cultural, and international backgrounds, as they represent the diverse faces of entrepreneurship today.

Seeking to illuminate and demystify the "unknown unknowns" that generate feelings of uncertainty and insecurity in new entrepreneurs, I asked founders about blind spots, unexpected lessons, what they would have done differently or wish they had known earlier, and how they handled moments of doubt. Importantly, I continued rounds of interviews until founders consistently shared similar tactics, advice, and wisdom.

I also use the term "startup" broadly, to include for-profit, nonprofit, and social enterprises that are working with a sense of urgency, where time is a valuable commodity and whose idealistic and imaginative founders have relinquished sometimes more stable or more lucrative opportunities in order to pursue their unique visions and dreams.

Finally, the book is written in "tip" form in order to emphasize the discrete principles of the entrepreneurial process and also to be as readable and accessible as possible for busy founders. If any of the tips seem obvious, don't be fooled. The founders I interviewed attribute their startup success to the ideas and advice contained in these pages. The simplicity of these ideas underscores the reality that startups aren't mysteries. They are created by hard work, they follow a certain process, and with some luck and good timing, you can be well assured that you are doing most things "right."

The process of being a founder will change you in the way that going to college or getting your first full-time job or getting married fundamentally transforms your sense of self and your perspectives on life. While founding an enterprise can be a daunting and frustrating process, the steps offered here will help you to launch and lead your startup, an experience that promises to be an enriching and life-changing journey.

PART ONE

HOW TO START

HOW TO START

I have a few ideas. How should I pick the best idea from the many that I have? I have been toying with one idea but I'm daunted by the task of making it "real." I also don't have many financial resources to devote to the startup. How do I move from idea to launch with limited resources?

When I was 28, I had the idea to establish a global women's leadership university for women from Asia and the Middle East. But I wasn't sure how I should start or what were the right steps to take. There were no books on the topic, and while I talked to academics helping to establish the Yale-NUS campus in Singapore or the NYU campus in Abu Dhabi, they had only come on board after these institutions were already well-funded government initiatives. I didn't feel their situations were similar to mine: they weren't single individuals with just an idea, starting from scratch and without ready access to capital. In addition, they weren't relatively young and un-established as I was in my career. But common sense dictated that any new brick-and-mortar university project would require four things: land for the campus, a host country, an academic partner, and a financial backer. These goals gave our startup comfort and focus. You may find yourself in a similar situation. To create structure and to anchor your efforts, begin by identifying central pillars, and then nibble away. These are the first crucial steps that will gradually transform your ideas into reality.

∞◦∞

Tip #1: Pin Down What You Want to Do

The first step is often the hardest, especially if you have a number of ideas and you are unsure which has the most promise. Here are the ways you can begin to pin down the first iteration of your startup idea:

1. **Generate a list of potential startup ideas, starting with what interests you.** Many founders come up with ideas based on their own desire for something that they themselves would want to use or buy. For example, Michael Schmidt of Vaska Technologies founded his company with a co-worker from GE. His company develops and designs smart home technologies that automatically reorder household consumables. He came up with this idea in the shower, when he found that he had run out of shampoo! He was annoyed that he would need to get dressed and leave the house simply to run the single errand of replenishing his shampoo, a task that could consume at least thirty minutes of his day. As he thought of how to avoid this problem in the future, he considered a monthly Amazon subscription but decided that there was a better solution. In short, his "pain point" became the source for his startup idea. You can use your own pain points as inspiration for new ideas.

2. **Pick the best idea that meets *each* of the following four criteria: passion, positioning, sustainability, and bandwidth.** These four criteria will be essential for the success of the startup. Pivots are always possible down the road, but deciding what you want to do and committing to the most promising idea at the moment is the first step in becoming an entrepreneur.

   - *Passion* ensures that when your energy wanes from time to time, and it will, other priorities will not eclipse your attention and commitment to your startup.
   - *Positioning* is whether you feel reasonably confident that you understand the startup space you might be entering and have an initial set of relevant contacts.
   - *Sustainability* is how your startup will generate income when it is in operation, regardless of whether it is for-profit or nonprofit. You must have a reasonable vision at the outset of

how your business model will eventually generate income. If you don't, your startup may be a hobby, but it will not be an enterprise.

- **Bandwidth** is how much time and how many resources you can realistically devote to your startup. You must be honest with yourself about this. No matter how good your idea is, you must truly have enough time and energy to give it what it needs in order for it to succeed.

Do not worry about choosing the perfect concept. No matter what you choose, your concept will almost certainly evolve or even transform over time. Pick an idea so that you can get moving on the startup process, and expect to make improvements, adjustments, and pivots along the way.

Tip #2: Identify Your Central Pillars

Once you have your startup idea, you must obtain a rough understanding of your plan for success. This can be hard because you'll have a blank canvas, and the final shape of your successful venture may not be obvious or prescribed. To structure your startup efforts, identify four central "pillars" – the most essential elements that your startup must achieve in order to stand on its own. Base them on common sense, as there is no exact science on the how to launch your startup. The aim is for the pillars to guide your efforts, and to help you understand the building blocks you require for your startup to operate. Later they will serve as **milestones of achievement** and markers of your progress.

For example, Ben Rubin co-founded the Change Collective, a company that helps people make changes in lifestyle, fitness, health, and productivity through mobile and online courses. By combining data, reminders, and social accountability tools, the company helps subscribers to follow through on changes they want to make in their lives. He realized that for these types of mobile and online courses to blossom into a successful business, he would need at least four critical elements: course content, a mobile/online streaming platform, expert coaches, and subscribers. These items formed the "four pillars," or foundational elements, of launching his business. He would also need to do many other things, such as write a business plan, develop a pricing model for the courses, and raise money. But identifying his four pillars was a crucial step in developing a strategy for his startup efforts.

The art of the start is identifying a few basic and key priorities (or pillars), and letting those priorities guide your initial efforts.

Tip #3: Nibble Away

Once you have identified your central pillars, you will need to break these ideas down into the nitty-gritty. People sometimes feel overwhelmed or lost when they focus only on the big idea and the ultimate vision of the startup, rather than on the series of **small steps** that will move you, little by little, toward the big idea's realization. How do you break down a big idea into small tasks and nibble away? Nibbling away means approaching each central pillar with small, actionable steps that help to achieve that milestone. It is about **direction and progress**, not magnitude.

Returning to our previous example, Ben Rubin's company, the Change Collective, offers lifestyle change courses through mobile and web technology. He had identified the development of course content as one of four central pillars that would be critical to the company's success. Building this one pillar required a series of actions: (i) drawing up a list of courses fitted to popular interest that could be taught online (such as fitness, dieting, and meditation), (ii) identifying experts in each of those fields, and (iii) emailing these experts to gauge their interest in partnering with his company. These actions constituted "nibbling away" at the major task of developing course content. As you get involved in accomplishing these small deeds, they will generate their own momentum and will reveal additional priorities that you will need to address. For example, Ben realized that in order to reach out effectively to the experts, he would need to develop an initial concept paper and a preliminary mock structure for his courses, so those became his next actions to complete.

As you nibble way, you won't find any pre-existing instructions on exactly what to do at each step because what you will be doing will be innovative and new. So don't worry about the one right thing to do at each step; focus instead on what seems reasonable and begin measuring success by your movement towards your central pillars.

NIBBLE AWAY:

Don't be daunted! The large magnitude of your startup idea is achieved through piece-by-piece completion of nibbling tasks: Take one of the central milestones of your startup, and with common sense, identify tasks that move you in the direction of achieving that milestone. These tasks will become your to-do list.

Tip #4: Start With What You Have

Young founders often wonder how to launch a startup, especially with limited manpower and financial resources. But don't despair; there are ways to start on a shoestring budget through volunteer networks and web-based resources.

1. **Recruit idealistic volunteers instead of hiring a startup team.** Reach out to family, friends, colleagues and college students who might want to get involved with your project, or who will at least spread the word of the opportunity to get in on the ground floor of an exciting new venture. From this pool of extended contacts, you can recruit interns, advisors, co-founders, board members, and maybe even investors. At first, though, it will be a team of energetic and dedicated volunteers.

    A well-chosen startup team can provide free legal, financial, and technical expertise that might otherwise cost thousands of dollars. A lawyer can review contracts, a financial analyst can produce financial and budget models, and an engineer can design prototypes for your startup. (*See also Tip #26 on how to seek out co-founders for your startup.*)

    Be aware that once you recruit board members and investors, you will likely have to cede some control to these individuals in order to benefit from their energy and expertise. You will have to persuade, negotiate, and occasionally compromise, rather than command. The value of talented collaborators is incalculable, however, and worth the loss of absolute control.

2. **Use virtual collaboration tools.** Meeting in person is often unnecessary and expensive. In order to avoid the costs of transportation, accommodation, and travel time, communicate online using programs such as Google Hangouts, Skype, Join.Me, Freeconferencecall.com, Slack.com, or Basecamp.com. These programs will allow you to conduct virtual conversations, demonstrations, and screen shares at little or no cost. New methods of online communication are constantly developing and improving. Seek out the latest and most efficient communication tools and take full advantage of them.

3. **Purchase online libraries of resources**. You can buy access to image libraries such as Istockphoto.com, Shutterstock.com and Depositphotos.com. You can even obtain free stock photos from sites such as Picography.co, Unsplash.com and Isorepublic.com. Using these resources for your publications, advertisements, and websites will be much less expensive than hiring a photographer to do a shoot or taking several days to do the shoot yourself. You can also buy access to professional pitch deck libraries (such as Slidevana.com) so that your investor or potential partnership presentations look professional. You can also purchase lists of companies operating in an industry that you may want to market or advertise to, instead of hiring sales and marketing people to generate such lists for you.

4. **Make simple websites and other media on your own.** Rather than hiring a web designer, try Wordpress.org, Wix.com, Fatcow.com, Squarespace.com, or Weebly.com, each of which offers ready-made templates that you can easily use to create a website. You can also create a Facebook page for your startup, and you can further publicize your startup by making your own 60-second video with simple templates available at PowToon.com, Animoto.com, or Moovly.com. You don't need coding, web development, web design, or graphic design skills. Instead, these easy-to-use platforms will enable you to present and publicize your startup until you are ready for (and can afford) a more sophisticated website and other forms of media.

5. **Outsource projects to online freelancers**. Rather than working alone or hiring a whole startup team, try freelance sources such as Mechanical Turk by Amazon, Upwork.com, Fiverr.com, Crowdflower.com, Freelancer.com, Spare5.com, Guru.com, or CloudFactory.com. Use inexpensive online labor for manual, clerical, or repetitive tasks to save the valuable time and energy of your existing team. You can also hire inexpensive technical experts, such as graphic designers who can create logos, websites, brochures and flyers for you in just a few days. Moreover, when you need quick and significant feedback on detailed aspects of your product line, it might be practical to ask friends and family who sometimes take a long time to respond or only assist at their convenience. For a modest amount, freelancers can provide you the quick user feedback that you need.

6. **Google search for solutions to your frustrations**: Don't reinvent the wheel. If something is taking a long time and you wonder if it could be done more easily or with an available technology, Google it. For example, you might find yourself wishing for a more efficient way to schedule appointments. If you Google search "scheduling and appointment software," you will learn about Any.do (which is free) among other scheduling solutions. Whenever you are working on a distinct aspect of your startup, such as writing a business plan, preparing an effective pitch deck, or trying to make a video go viral, Google that topic online to gather quick tips and the wisdom floating out on the web.

    For example, Google searching on topics such as ticketing customer service requests (Zendesk), managing relationships with prospective clients (Infusionsoft), monitoring what employees are working on (Hubstaff), accounting software (Quickbook Cloud), and tracking email communications (Yesware) will reveal a variety of solutions that you may not have known about.

Manik Suri, for example, was accustomed to having a lot of support and resources when he worked in the private sector and when he co-founded a well-funded nonprofit called the Governance Lab. However, when he founded his next venture, MeWe (a technology start-up that builds software to simplify regulation and streamline compliance), he was surprised to find that he could accomplish nearly all of his startup goals even without the costly support and resources that had been available to him in his previous ventures. Manik used online freelancers to beta test his prototypes and substantially reduced travel costs through the virtual collaboration tools mentioned earlier.

Don't worry that you don't have everything that you need at the outset. Start with what you have – and everyone has friends and family that you can turn to for initial support. As we'll see in the next tip, you also have your own talents that you can count on.

DO-IT-YOURSELF:

DIY: Turning to family, friends, and volunteers, and using efficient and inexpensive online tools, allows you to advance your startup idea even on a limited budget. With these tools, you'll be able to accomplish much of what you set out to do, even without being an expert in any task.

Tip #5: De-emphasize the Importance of Expertise

As a founder, you will be stepping into the unknown and building as you go. You will have to wear multiple hats, not all of which will be familiar or comfortable for you. It's okay not to know everything right away, since being an entrepreneur is a constant learning process. Don't stall your startup out of fear that you don't know how to do something.

1. **Give yourself permission to go ahead and do it yourself, even if you do not have professional training or expertise**. Many new founders are surprised by what they can accomplish when they try something they have never done before.

   For example, Joshua Redstone, founder of Equatine Labs, wanted to file a patent for his invention of a more precise measuring cup. At first he didn't know whether his product was worthy of a patent, and he wondered if he would need to hire a lawyer to complete the patent application. Seeking to contain costs, he downloaded a patent application online, read the instructions, and filled out the application on his own. Only then did he pay a lawyer to review his patent application, so as to ensure that it explicitly conveyed the novelty of his invention. By diving in and doing it himself, he saved money and time.

2. **Don't let your lack of legal knowledge stop you from incorporating your startup as a legal entity**. Each state has an office to support new nonprofit organizations and for-profit businesses. You can find out how to incorporate a company or a nonprofit by calling your state's Small Business Administration office. You can also consult websites such as Score.org, which provides resources for small businesses and startups. The career services offices at most universities have someone on staff to talk to you about starting your own business or to point you to helpful resources.

   Law schools will often offer pro bono clinics to support startups. Check local law schools and see if they offer such a program. Law firms (such as WilmerHale, Goodwin Procter, Venture Law Group, or Fenwick and West) may ask for a small equity stake in your company or defer legal fees until you raise venture money. As Jamie Beaton (founder of Crimson Consulting, a college test prep and admissions company) says,

"Professional services should always be negotiated down, since you're really just paying for someone's time. Check quotes and hustle to get prices down." In fact, you should seek out not only deferred payments, but also a discount on the legal fees themselves.

As a founder you will need to dip your toes into diverse professional domains, including fundraising, web design, and human resource management, just to name a few. Don't worry that you are not formally trained in these areas. Embrace the opportunity to be a generalist and celebrate that, by doing so, you are experiencing one of the hallmarks of entrepreneurship. Before taking on any of these roles, however, there is one broad question that you will need to address: what sort of incorporation should you pursue?

Tip #6: Incorporate as a For-Profit or a Nonprofit

Many entrepreneurs, especially those with idealistic and socially responsible goals, seek incorporation as a nonprofit. A for-profit venture may seem more daunting to initiate, since you must demonstrate the startup's reasonable potential to generate profit. However, keep in mind that a nonprofit venture also has hurdles and challenges:

1. **Even a nonprofit startup must be able to generate income.** Any organization will need to generate income to function whether it does so through donations or by selling a product or service (*see Tip #1 regarding the need to identify a reasonable strategy for how your startup will earn income to sustain operations*). The difference is that in for-profits, any profit can be pocketed by the owners of the company, whereas in a nonprofit, excess income must be plowed back into the company. Both, however, must make income in some form to survive!

2. **Pitching a nonprofit startup will be especially challenging.** Although it may seem easier to found a nonprofit, potential investors or contributors will have no financial incentive (other than a possible tax deduction) to invest in or contribute to a nonprofit venture. If your startup is for-profit, however, it may actually be far easier to pitch a potential financial gain to a prospective investor. A for-profit founder will also stand to gain financially from her efforts, and will likely retain more control, since she will own a definitive equity stake in the company.

3. **As a nonprofit, you will not stand to gain financially from your efforts.** You also will make significant sacrifices of time, money, relationships, and reputation for which you may not otherwise be compensated or recognized. If your nonprofit gets established as a 501(c)(3) nonprofit charity with its own board of directors, it becomes an organization that ultimately is not yours to own. Instead, the board of directors of a nonprofit holds ultimate authority. Each board member will have exactly one vote, regardless of how much or how little time, money, or other

resource each member has invested. Board fights do happen, even among those with the best intentions. You can be ousted from your role and your history in the founding of the organization can also be erased (*see Tip #68 on expecting conflict*).

For-profit founders can also be ousted from their companies (remember Steve Jobs's ouster from Apple?), but they will at least retain their financial stake in the company. Your nonprofit startup will feel like your baby. Once you achieve nonprofit status, however, the board of directors essentially adopts your baby. This can be a difficult reality for a founder of a nonprofit to accept.

4. **Consider carefully whether you are choosing to incorporate as a nonprofit because it is "easier" or whether there are other compelling reasons to do so.** Consider getting legal advice (by consulting online resources such as Startuplawyer.com, finding a lawyer on Linkilaw.com, or Google searching startup law firms in your area) to help you think through ownership and control issues and how they might be spelled out in stockholder agreements and organizational documents.

After you have figured out how to incorporate your startup, it's time to get the word out.

FOR-PROFIT VS. NONPROFIT:

Both for-profits and nonprofits have to make revenue! What are the pros and cons of each?

– **For-profit founders** must present a business model that shows how the startup is able to generate income and profit but can pitch investors a potential financial upside in exchange for taking on a risky business model.

– **Nonprofit founders** do not have to demonstrate how the startup will turn a profit, but face the difficulty of convincing others to invest in the startup when those individuals have no prospect of financial gain.

Tip #7: Get It Out the Door

Don't let perfectionism keep you from getting an idea out the door, even if it still needs some tweaking or even substantial revision. Worry less about how ready you are to launch your startup and more about developing a first, imperfect version so you can collect feedback and start fine-tuning your idea (or scrapping the initial idea and pivoting as necessary).

1. **Release your "minimum viable product" (MVP).** Whenever you can show something to someone, get their thoughts, and figure out what they like and don't like, you should consider it your MVP. It doesn't matter if your MVP is as simple as a paragraph-long email of your idea, a hand drawn mockup of what you want to offer, an in-progress website, or an initial prototype. It can be *anything* that allows you to get initial feedback on your idea.

2. **Check various prototyping tools to help you present your idea.** Many platforms such as Balsamiq.com, InVisionapp.com, or Autocad allow you to present your startup idea as realistically as possible and even if it is still in design stages.

3. **Be less concerned about the imperfections of your product or service.** Rather than viewing your initial prototype as an unfinished product, see it as a first necessary step on the road to discovering your potential customers' true pain points. Getting the feedback to guide future improvements will serve your business in the long run. Creating products and sharing improvements quickly also gives you ample room to impress others with your progress.

Omar Abudayyeh, the co-founder of Modalyst, an e-commerce platform for retailers to connect with independent brands, shared this experience with his first startup: He was in charge of product development while his co-founder was in charge of graphics. He and his co-founder initially experienced tension when his co-founder wanted to launch a basic version of their website while Omar wanted to delay the launch of the site so he could improve its functionality. The tension was eventually resolved when they agreed to launch a minimal viable product (a "beta" version) to a select group of customers. Since then Modalyst has iterated multiple aesthetic makeovers and launched two major product features for customers.

As Omar says, *"It looks and feels so much different than our initial product and customers love it. I now understand the need to iterate early. You don't want to spend a year developing a product only to find that no one is using it. You want to be aware of who you are developing for and why and get their feedback as early as possible."*

Once you have something to show someone, you'll need to actually show it. The next chapter shares ideas of how to approach others, talk about your startup idea, and pitch yourself and your idea to others.

PART TWO

HOW TO PITCH YOUR IDEA AND ESTABLISH CREDIBILITY

HOW TO PITCH YOUR IDEA
AND ESTABLISH CREDIBILITY

I've been working on my idea and now I want to start sharing it with other people. I admit, however, that I feel self-conscious about being fairly young and I don't have much experience and I haven't run my own company before. What's the most effective way to share my startup idea and establish credibility so people take me seriously?

When I wanted to share the idea for an Asian Women's Leadership University with a wider audience, I wasn't sure how to present it. In particular, my insecurities rose to the surface: Who was I to be so audacious as to imagine establishing a university, and how naïve was I to try in earnest to do it? I already felt that I was attempting to the do the near impossible, and that people would view me as foolish. Would it be better to say with gusto that I was trying to establish the AWLU or to tentatively suggest that I was merely thinking about it? I also often felt self-conscious about how young I looked, especially given the magnitude of the project I was taking on. As a result of these insecurities, I wondered if I should wait to share the idea until I had made substantial progress and could more credibly proclaim my vision. You may similarly feel that you don't have enough traction to share your idea or that you don't know the best way to talk about your startup while it is still developing. The tips below, however, encourage you to share your startup idea and suggest strategies for strengthening the confidence others have in your startup efforts (including your own), even when you feel self-conscious or, at times, in over your head.

Tip #8: Ask for Help with the Royal "We"

People are often reluctant to eat at a restaurant with just one lonely patron, no matter how good the meal might actually be. They want to eat at a bustling restaurant. When you use the royal "we," you serve up the image of a bustling organization.

As a startup, your initial team will be small and perhaps will consist only of you. Yet you'll be trying to drum up support and visibility. Instead of saying "*I am trying to develop an app that allows kids to do math problems and earn their parents' allowance,*" or "*I am now in the process of raising seed funding,*" say "*We are developing an app…*" or "*We are in the process of raising seed funding.*" This **switch from singular to plural** suggests a level of gravity and significance to your work. Ventures where more than one person is involved are also more likely to garner support, and you can make that first step towards growth by saying "We" from the start. This pronoun also makes it easier for you to talk to and seek assistance from others, since it will feel less personal for others if they are not able to support your venture (*see Tip #20 on the importance of giving easy outs*).

But don't just pretend that you have a posse. Actually have one and show that you do.

Tip #9: Get Social Proof

With so many startups out there, you'll need to distinguish your startup from other ones and enhance the credibility of your venture. One way to do so is to garner positive and public mentions from credible sources about what your startup is doing. This is known as "social proof." Get the word out in digital (or real) print so that when people search for your organization or your name online, third-party content appears. Media visibility will increase interest and confidence in your venture.

Here are some proactive ways to get visibility and positive third-party commentary about what you're doing:

1. **Seek out endorsements from credible entities and individuals whose needs your startup addresses.** For example, Canopy Apps creates an app that helps doctors and patients communicate more easily by providing quick translations of medical terms and instructions during patient visits. To obtain social proof, Jerrit Tan, the CEO, reached out to various medical associations and sought their endorsement of the app so he could leverage their endorsement with their membership base. He also sought testimonials from individual users willing to share their positive feedback.

2. **Search online for articles addressing issues that are related to your startup, and then track down the writers of those articles.** Writers and publications are always looking for new content to showcase. If you let them know what your startup is doing, they might decide to write about it. Often the bottom of the article will indicate the writer's email or other contact information. (*See also Tip #50 on how to obtain email contact information even when it isn't readily available on the web.*) Getting bigger magazines, newspapers, and social media outlets to cover your startup is ideal, but articles by smaller publications (such as an alumni magazine, school newspaper, local paper, industry newsletter, professional association newsletter, or even someone's blog) are immensely worthwhile.

3. **Individual and organizational affiliations also serve as social proof.** Seek out ways to affiliate with an institution, such as your college, your alma mater, an investing group, or a startup

incubator. You can even create your own advisory council with two or three well-known persons in your startup space. (*See Tip #37 on how to recruit advisors for your startup.*) People want to know that you are not working alone and that you have other existing supporters who are willing to publically associate with and vouch for you.

It is great to get others to talk about your startup. You can pull your weight, too, and talk up the startup yourself.

Tip #10: Create Your Own Publicity

While you will want to nudge others to spotlight your startup, don't wait for others to initiate public outreach. Create visibility and build authority in your startup domain by publishing ideas yourself. Here are several points to consider in creating a buzz for your startup or idea:

1. **Start writing down your ideas, drawing them if you have to, and publishing them – even if it's a blog post on your startup's website.** For example, Zac Aghion, the founder of Splitforce, created a company that makes A/B testing software (allowing clients to test two different versions of mobile applications and see which one is performing better). He attributes the success and subsequent sale of his company to writing down his ideas and publishing them in a blog post.

   As Zac says, "*Many people have many ideas, but not many people document and promote their ideas. There's a huge leap from having an idea or recognizing a trend or a vision for the future, and actually documenting and sharing that with others. What makes someone an expert is having a thought and sharing it with the world.*"

   Don't set the bar higher than that: you don't need a PhD in the subject. If you have a perspective on an issue or have found a problem and identified a potential solution, share it through the internet (such as Medium.com) or social media. You can also go the traditional route through a physical medium such as a book, pamphlet, or DVD.

2. **Hire someone else to write down your idea and attribute it back to you.** For example, Zac hired freelancers to search out and answer questions on the Internet about A/B testing in his and his company's name. Zac would provide a set of content and allow the freelancer to pick and choose from the content to answer questions about A/B testing on the Internet. The freelancer would then attribute the answer back to Splitforce and to Zac. Thus, Zac's company became more well-known within industry circles, and Zac became an expert in A/B testing, someone who was sought after to speak at conferences and for consulting opportunities.

With a few ideas about how to get the word out, be prepared to keep doing it again, and again, and again.

Tip #11: Pitch, Pitch, Pitch

Many young founders are afraid to pitch their idea because they don't feel established enough to rave about their startup. They are also afraid of public failure. Despite this discomfort, you should nevertheless make sure that everyone you meet knows what you are working on. While many of these people will not be actively involved in your startup, more than you expect will have some relevant knowledge, insights, or contacts that might help to advance your venture.

As a result of your persistent pitching, you will establish connections, obtain potential help, and get feedback that might inform how you develop your startup idea. Individuals may suggest conferences you can speak at, or refer you to others, or refer others to you. In addition, each time you describe your project, you gain practice in refining your pitch and anticipating common reactions. Talking with others about your startup also solidifies your own commitment. Share your idea widely and be surprised by the results. (See also Oren Klaff's *Pitch Anything*.)

When crafting your pitch, have these points in mind:

1. **Your initial pitch should be a short, 10-second elevator pitch.** You should be able to describe your startup so that others can understand what you are doing very quickly. If people do not have a clear sense of what you are trying to do from this one sentence, you will need to revise your pitch. Don't try to be fancy or use technical words. Just get to the meat of your startup idea and keep it simple. For example, our pitch for the AWLU Project was *"to establish a global leadership university for women from Asia and the Middle East. Our aim is to cultivate a cadre of women leaders to advance social, political, and economic development in the region."*

2. **Pitch even when you're not sure someone can help.** Pitch in social situations, in professional situations, at school, at family gatherings – everywhere. You never know who might be able to help or what connections may exist within your network. Consider the case of Arabella Simpkin, the founder of Greyscale Spaces, a professional development company that trains workers to deal with ambiguity. As a physician, she recognized that doctors often work under conditions of uncertainty and imperfect

data, so she was initially targeting medical professionals. However, she happened to have a conversation with a detective and chief inspector of a police department and learned that police encounter a lot of ambiguity, such as when they do stops and searches, and must also make decisions on imperfect data. By sharing her idea widely, Arabella was invited to do a training session with new police cadets and has now opened her business beyond the medical sphere.

3. **Don't worry that by sharing your idea you expose yourself to others who might copy or take your idea.** Few people are willing to take the time for such an endeavor. It will be more beneficial for you to get reactions and feedback to your idea, accelerating the hole-poking process so you can expose and address the weaknesses (or opportunities) in your idea. You may consider the benefits and drawbacks of pursuing a nondisclosure or confidentiality agreement (NDA) if there are times when you will want to be very careful about the information that you share. (For example, Google search Orrick.com's Startup Tool Kit, which includes a model NDA and other helpful template documents. Overwhelmingly, however, do not be concerned at all that someone will "take" or "steal" your idea. Ideas are less consequential than the implementation. It's easy to have good ideas; it's very hard to actually work steadfastly on them.

4. **Search online for how to make the pitch deck and what should be included in your presentation.** Before formally presenting a pitch deck to an investor or at a pitch competition, take a look at Crowdfunder.com's investor pitch deck template, or Google search other templates. You'll learn how much time to use, and how many slides to include. You'll also learn that you should tell a story rather than just convey facts. Importantly, the aim of the pitch deck is not to answer all possible questions, but to excite supporters to learn more. (*See also Tip #32 about not drowning people with information.*)

5. **Don't expect the pitch to secure an immediate investment; the follow-up conversation does.** Many new founders think that after the pitch, the audience will immediately indicate a response, when in fact, most will be left with only a general impression,

positive or negative. Most likely they will not be ready to make a decision, so asking them to decide right away would make them uncomfortable. Instead, tell your audience that you hope they saw potential in your idea and an alignment with their objectives. Tell them you will give them some time to think over your plan, and that you will follow up with them in the coming days or weeks. Be mindful that an effective pitch is comprised of more than just the pitch itself and is the product of relationship cultivation, pitch presentation, and a well-paced follow-up process. (*See also Tip #63 about using a four-steps-or-fewer fundraising process.*)

Now that you have plenty to say, you will need something to show for all that effort, letting people see and remember what you do.

PITCH IT STRAIGHT:

Don't get fancy with your pitch. Just tell people exactly what you are trying to do (e.g. "we sell kale candy bars"). The faster you can convey what you're working on, the easier it will be for others to suggest potential contacts or resources. You might develop a 10-second, 30-second, minute-long, or two-minute elevator pitch. But write the 10-second one first.

Tip #12: Show, Don't Tell

Make your startup as tangible and visible as possible. Attract the support and confidence of others through pictures, graphics, slide decks, charts, posters, a logo, business cards, a rough prototype, customized tee shirts, or even a memorable gimmick. Such items will show people where you are in the startup process and what you have already accomplished, and they will spark people's imagination about where your startup will go in the future.

For example, Michele Lunati, the founder of Potluck Energy, was looking to recruit a talented startup team to help him launch a community solar farm. To convey his vision for and the feasibility of this large-scale project, he visited the manufacturing plant of a solar power project developer and took pictures of the solar panels and the technical equipment used to build them. He also took pictures of local community members signing-up to learn more about participating in a community solar farm energy program, as well as the sign-up sheet itself. Through these images and despite the initial daunting nature of his startup idea, he was able to recruit a high caliber co-founding team to work with him.

People are visual creatures. Don't underestimate the power of pictures to inspire support and confidence. Whenever you can, show pictures of your startup activities to convey your vision, your path to success, and the progress you have already made. But not only will you need to show people what your startup is doing, you'll also need to tell a public narrative of why you are doing it.

PICTURES ARE WORTH 1,000 WORDS:

Don't overload your pitch with words! Use graphics, drawings, photos, charts, slides, and other visuals. Pictures make your presentation catchy, sustain attention, and don't overwhelm your prospective investor with too much information!

Tip #13: Craft Your Public Narrative

Any startup's feasibility will be subject to some doubt, so don't let people pile on additional skepticism because they don't understand who you are or where you are coming from. Before launching into the specifics of your startup, share what motivated you and why you care about your startup idea. Marshall Ganz is a professor at the Harvard Kennedy School. Each year he teaches hundreds of students about leadership in a course called "Public Narrative," where students learn that the way to mobilize and inspire support is by articulating who you are, including your values and the source of those values. Here are some ways you can help craft your narrative:

1. **Prepare and offer a public account of who you are.** Especially when you are working on a social cause, you must offer, implicitly or explicitly, a public account of who you are and why you are doing what you are doing. Whether you are a for-profit or a nonprofit founder, you will need to explain not only what market need you are filling, but also how you came up with your startup idea and why you are personally motivated and uniquely suited to spend the necessary time and energy on your venture. People may not actually ask you these questions, but you can be sure that they are listening for the answers anyhow. Be prepared to articulate a deeply personal account of your motivations.

2. **Engage in a process of self-reflection to identify your values**. This is part of the emotional work that you'll do as a founder of your own startup, and it may be uncomfortable. To start this process of self-reflection, consider the following questions: What challenges have you faced? How did you overcome them? What choices did you make about the college or graduate program you went to, the activities you spent your time on, the experiences that you sought out, or the career that you chose to pursue? You might also consider what made your parents the people they became, or reflect on how their choices or their experiences influenced your own. Try to recall specific events that changed how you thought about your interests and your strengths, and consider why you were drawn to a certain activity over another. Reflecting on these questions should illuminate your values and how they conect to your startup.

3. **Practice telling your narrative until answering questions about how you became motivated to work on your startup becomes easy and natural.** Once you have thought about your motivations for your startup and talked with some trusted people about them, you will be ready to tell your public narrative and commit to your startup effort. This is important because in nearly every meeting, themes from your personal life and values will emerge.

Don't think that people aren't interested, that your story doesn't matter or isn't relevant, or that you shouldn't be talking about yourself. In fact, authenticity will form the foundation for all the work that you do for your startup, as experts such as Marshall Ganz have long recognized that persons – not projects alone – inspire support. Once you have your own story down, you'll need to tell the story of your business.

Tip #14: Use Business Plans as Stories

Entrepreneurs tend to stress about the business plan and especially about the financial model of their startup. They are worried about getting it "right" as if there were a correct way to write one. A business plan is just a roadmap for your business that outlines goals and details how you plan to achieve those goals. It need not be a long, formal document.

Don't worry so much about the business plan, especially since most people, investors included, would rather view a shorter and more concise pitch deck. Writing a business plan is useful, however, as an exercise to make sure you have thoroughly thought out your startup idea. This thorough planning enables you to make a pitch deck as well as to discuss the startup in greater detail. Your ability to "talk the details" will be part of what gains you respect and credibility. The business plan will also serve as the central warehouse that stores and organizes the research you have done. (See also Lena Ramfelt, Jonas Kjellberg, and Tom Kosnik's *Gear Up* and Alexander Osterwalder and Yves Pigneur's *Business Model Generation*.)

To make the business plan work for you, consider the following:

1. **View the business plan as a *persuasive document* rather than a factual one.** It should tell a story and make an argument that (a) you have a thorough understanding of how to start and operate your enterprise, and (b) your enterprise is a promising venture (meeting a market or social need), and therefore worthy of support and investment. While there is no single way to write a business plan, don't hesitate to search online for examples that are relevant to your industry. At the same time, you should feel great liberty to customize the content and format of your business plan so that it reflects your startup's unique aspects. Pictures of the team, prototypes, mock-ups, or startup activities can also be included.

2. **In general, a business plan will consist of many logically connected parts:**

   - executive summary
   - a description of your enterprise (what your company does or will do)

- the market opportunity or value proposition (what needs are not being met currently)
- product or service features
- a survey of the competitive landscape
- a description of any proof of concept (outcomes of early trials, focus group testing, market surveys, or adoption rates)
- initial funding plans
- a financial plan (that reflects the funding required to support your future activities and expected income and expenditure streams)
- a sales and marketing strategy (who your customers are and how you will find them)
- a plan of execution (the milestones you hope to achieve and the timeline for achieving them)
- details on the startup team (bios of team members, including board members or advisors)
- organizational structure (an organizational chart detailing roles and reporting lines)

Writing the business plan and addressing each of these discrete areas is useful because it requires you to anticipate how you will carry out your business. It will serve not only as a marketing document, but also as a handy roadmap for future operations.

3. **Financial projections are guaranteed to be inaccurate. So don't sweat it.** Of all the parts of the business plan, the financial plan detailing the amounts needed to support future activities (based on projected income and expenditure streams in the short and long term) often causes the most distress to founders. They are concerned about the accuracy of the numbers it includes. These projections, however, do not need to be precisely accurate. Instead, you should make sure that your financial projections are *sensible* and based on a number of **reasonable and defensible assumptions** (you should create a separate assumptions tab). As long as you are explicit and clearly understand the basis of these assumptions, then your financial plan can become a tool to convince investors and others to support your startup. In addition, your financial model should note:

- When you expect to earn your first revenue (make your first sale)
- When you expect to break even (revenue covers cost of operating)
- When you expect to generate profit (income exceeds expenses)

When you are driving along a windy road at night, your headlights allow you to see just what is ahead of you. Financial projections are similar. While the financial plan should be highly detailed regarding the first three years of operations, it's also fine that the level of specificity wanes as your projections extend beyond that timeframe.

4. **To help you tackle the business plan, try filling out applications for pitch competitions or startup incubators.** Even if you don't think you'll be accepted or if you think you're not ready or don't have enough time to submit an application, filling out application forms will force you to concretize your strategy and to answer questions that should be addressed by the business plan, such as your beachhead market entry point (that is, the first market that you will choose to pursue), your customer target and profile, and what market research you have done. Having to develop your elevator pitch also forces you to think about and present the crux of your idea.

Your business plan needn't present a thoroughly accurate prediction of the future. It must merely paint a convincing picture of what you are trying to do, how you will try to do it, and what you know about the landscape that your startup will be entering. As the paint is drying, you might also need to be ready to add another layer and adapt to new information. Plans change, so how will you react?

Tip #15: Don't Get So Stuck to the Idea

As an entrepreneur, you will need to balance your desire to preserve your original idea with the need to remain open and adaptive to feedback. Don't be so emotionally attached to your first idea that you are unwilling to allow your startup to evolve. There is merit to remaining steadfast and true to your vision, but you must also acknowledge when something is not working and be willing to shift your strategy or business altogether. When putting out your idea:

1. **Accept feedback and follow advice.** This sounds easy but it is actually very hard. When you share your startup idea, you'll receive a lot of reactions and responses. But undoubtedly you will have an emotional attachment to whatever previous idea or decision you have made. This attachment to earlier ideas can make it difficult to change even a logo or a name. While you don't have to accept every opinion as gospel, strive to rise above defensiveness. Instead, adopt a receptive stance, where you are open to and grateful for the perspectives of others: your mentors, your customers, your focus group, or even random people on the street. Consider implementing the changes that people suggest. It is crucial that you remain open to feedback, because there will be no one – no boss – to tell you what to do or to critique your performance.

2. **Prepare to reconsider your assumptions about what customers will like or about what constitutes a good idea**. For example, Roger Ying, the founder of Pandai.cn, a peer-to-peer lending platform in China, was upgrading his company's website. He found a Chinese designer with western design experience to create a clean, chic, and contemporary website. In focus group testing, however, Roger found that 70% of his Chinese clients disliked the new website, even though the old website was very busy and disorganized. He explored the reasons for the negative reaction and learned that web viewers in China preferred a busy and complicated website because it gave them a satisfying feeling that others were using the website at the same time, unlike a page with a clean but static design.

3. **Prepare to pivot your entire business**. Start with one idea, but expect it to evolve based on new information or challenges or

opportunities that you encounter. A founder's initial idea should never turn out to be the final product. Changing the idea – refining it, revising it, and sometimes abandoning it to pursue another more fruitful idea – is key to being an entrepreneur.

Frank Yao, the founder of Smith Street Solutions, readily admits that his consulting firm is very different today from the business graphics outsourcing company that he first envisioned and which helped Chinese companies convert hand drawn depictions into PowerPoint.

Once he set up his business, however, he learned that Indian outsourcing companies already provided these services at a level of quality and cost that were hard to match. He also realized that his Chinese employees were upwardly mobile. Since graphics work was repetitive, Frank found it hard to retain employees. However, even as his graphics outsourcing company was floundering, his clients would ask if his firm could also do primary and secondary data collection. While it took more than three years, Frank transformed his unsuccessful graphics outsourcing business into a successful consulting business.

Similarly, Lisa Walker, the founder of LearningInSync, wanted to have an impact on education in Tanzania. At first, she thought she could pursue this goal by creating a nonprofit that would develop and provide bilingual teaching materials in the country. While she did not find much success in fundraising for this project, she did receive numerous offers of consulting work for various existing educational projects in Tanzania.

Although she initially redoubled her efforts to seek out those interested in bilingual education materials, she eventually converted the focus of her nonprofit to consulting services related to the development and management of education projects in Tanzania. She didn't do what she initially set out to do, but by staying flexible, she accomplished her goal through another activity that was more successful. This is the kind of flexibility that you should aim for as well.

4. **Once you decide to pivot your startup idea, do it as swiftly as possible.** Pivot quickly to minimize angst and to focus resources on ensuring that the new business succeeds. For example, Frank Yao says, "*It took us three years to shift our business model, but the change could have been done in one day; but it takes a long time to*

execute on the right decision even though all the signs in your mind are telling you the right answer." Let the context have an impact on how you proceed. In particular, pay attention to and follow what the market is telling you, as it won't lie to you. You aren't doing yourself or your business partners any favors by dragging out what needs to be done. Of course, making a significant strategic change is hard, both fiscally and emotionally, and not all of your team members will be able to make the transition. When facing such difficult decisions, be sure to seek objective advice from people outside your startup.

5. **Remember, if you aren't pivoting, then you aren't learning.** If you find yourself always resisting change, or if your initial startup idea has not evolved significantly or at all, let that be a signal to you that you are not practicing enough flexibility and are not being open to learning. Learning involves change. It's very unlikely that you will have gotten everything right in the first iteration of your startup. When you do make a difficult change, throw a "pivot party" where you celebrate your change as evidence of your learning – and your success.

Once you have done some of the initial legwork of drumming up some confidence in your startup – by getting social proof and publicity, showing what you've accomplished, telling a compelling personal and business story of what you're trying to accomplish and why, incorporating early feedback and modifying your startup idea – you'll need to invite the involvement of others. The next chapter shares ideas of how you can effectively approach others to support your startup efforts.

REALITY CHECK:

When was the last time you made a change that you were less than totally comfortable with based on consistent advice or feedback? Don't get founders' passion blinders. Expect and celebrate uncomfortable changes to your idea. These changes will represent your learning and improve your startup idea.

PART THREE

HOW TO SEEK
AND OBTAIN
EARLY SUPPORT

HOW TO SEEK AND OBTAIN EARLY SUPPORT

What's the most effective way to engage others and ask for help? How do I get people to meet with me or to support my venture? How do I craft emails that will elicit positive responses? I also don't want to impose on others, but I do need assistance.

While I connected emotionally and intellectually with others over the need to establish the Asian Women's Leadership University, I often didn't know the best way to ask them for commitments of time, money, or affiliation. In many cases, I was not sure if I was asking for too much or too little, too quickly or not quickly enough. Asking for large donations also felt awkward. I hadn't learned yet to make smaller and well-paced asks and to give others gracious ways to decline my invitation to become involved. It was also disheartening to compose long, thoughtful emails and to get no replies. I had not yet mastered the art of crafting short, pithy emails that grabbed attention and generated responses. You may be experiencing similar frustrations. Fortunately there is a code to these early conversations. Once you learn the code and find a rhythm that works for you, you'll be able to solicit assistance confidently and appropriately, and to gracefully accept the disappointment even when some people inevitably say no.

Tip #16: Move from Pitch to Process

As you seek support for your startup, you should distinguish between a "pitch" and a "process." Initially, you will not know what is the most effective and efficient approach for obtaining media coverage, securing investors, recruiting board members, attracting talented employees, signing up new customers, or any number of other activities. As the founder, it will be your job to **experiment with multiple approaches** until you discover the one that works best for the task at hand.

Each attempted approach is just a "pitch." With a pitch, you are test-driving an approach that you think might be effective. Once you have systematically tried various approaches, however, you should discover the one that yields reliably positive responses. This approach will become your "process" for whatever you are doing – making sales, recruiting co-founders, recruiting employees, seeking endorsements, and so on. Thus, you must not only recognize at what point you've settled on the most effective pitch, but make it your job to find the most effective, well-edited, and well-practiced pitch so that it can become your "process."

For example, Mee-Jung Jang, the founder of Voncierge, an online appointment booking system for the bridal industry, was trying to sign up wedding vendors for her online wedding reservation system. After trying different approaches, she finally realized that the process that most reliably elicited reliably positive responses was to make an appointment at a wedding salon, as if she were an actual bride looking for a dress. At the appointment, she would ask the salesperson to introduce her to the owner and explain to the owner that she was looking for a wedding dress and was having a hard time booking appointments. She would ask about their appointment system, which she knew was still a paper appointment book. She would then mention that she wanted to create a website where brides could book appointments, and she wondered aloud if such a system might also benefit the salon, since the salespeople would not have to spend time making appointments and could thus devote more time to potential sales. The response was often positive, and she would get the vendor's contact information and sign up the vendor. She utilized this process to sign up vendors during the initial stages of her startup. Later, she switched to a more conventional sales process by making initial contact via a well-crafted email that also elicited a high response rate.

Once you find a sales process that "works" for your startup (including the most efficient process), you will be able to relax and trust the process. (At this point, you can assign a team member to apply that process at scale, and free yourself to solve other problems.) To develop an effective process, however, you'll need to know how to pace interactions and communications with others.

PITCH VS. PROCESS:

Keep experimenting with different pitches until you come across a process that "works."

- Pitch: when you try different approaches, hoping to convince someone. You are unsure what reactions might be and conversations feel high stakes.

Vs.

- Process: when you apply a method that yields reliable and positive results. You expect a range of responses, and are confident that at least some will be positive.

Tip #17: Distinguish Between Main and Incremental Asks

It is important for you to know exactly what you are seeking from any particular communication, and to pace your requests accordingly. There are many kinds of asks – to meet for coffee, to participate in a conference call, to get advice, to make a pitch, to hear feedback, to be introduced to someone, to get contact information, to ask for an endorsement, to get an investment, to recruit a board member, to recruit an advisor, and so on. Don't confuse one for another, as the type of ask will determine how you conduct yourself. Here are some ideas for keeping your asks clear:

1. **Your initial outreach email is not a pitch, but most likely a request for a call or meeting.** New founders often think of the outreach email as an opportunity to make a pitch – they fear that if they don't make a convincing pitch right then and there that they may lose the recipient's interest. But approaching potential stakeholders is like approaching a cat or a deer. You must do so gently and patiently, and always pace yourself. Any sudden movements might just scare them away. In your first email, you should only be asking for a meeting or a phone call, nothing more. At that stage you should merely try to whet the recipient's appetite for learning more about your startup. Your first objective is to merely secure the opportunity for a call or meeting.

2. **Distinguish between "main asks" and "incremental asks."** Keep in mind that for every "main ask," there are a number of "incremental asks" that lead up to the main ask.

   For example, your main ask might be *"Will you invest $100,000 in my start-up?"* But to get to that point, you'll need to make numerous smaller asks: for an initial call, for a meeting to describe the opportunity that your startup represents in more detail, for advice about the design of your product or service, or for a discussion about potential participation in your startup as an investor, before launching into a discussion about the actual level of a potential investment.

   Similarly, another main ask might be *"Would you be willing to join my board?"* Some incremental asks might be: to meet for a first coffee meeting to learn about your contact's relevant experiences, to meet for a second coffee to hear her advice on a specific challenge you are facing, and to serve as an advisor – all before you get to the main ask.

Being able to identify clearly what you are looking for at each stage of a relationship will help you to make the most relevant request for that moment and avoid making a premature or excessive request.

3. **Know which "ask" you plan to make for each proposed meeting, but be prepared to adjust the ask depending on the conversation.** Each time you request a meeting or call with someone, be sure you understand the specific purpose of each conversation. But also be ready to adjust your request depending on the tone, attitude, or extent of interest that your prospect conveys.

    For example, you may be going into a meeting with a purpose of making a pitch or soliciting an investor. However, if in the course of the conversation, you sense that the person is not interested in investing, you should shift your interaction. Instead of seeing the person as a lost source for financial support, see the person instead as a source of information or additional contacts. Be prepared to make these shifts as a conversation progresses. At each stage of the process, you can ask for a greater or lesser level of commitment based on the amount of encouragement and enthusiasm that you are feeling from a potential stakeholder.

Now that you know the basics about how to set up an ask, it's time to make that contact (usually through an email) and get the ball rolling.

TEE UP YOUR MAIN ASKS:

Don't rush the courtship process! Keep clear on your main asks and the incremental asks and the purpose for each. Let's say your Main Ask is a product endorsement of your app (with the contact's company logo and testimonial on your website). To tee up your main ask, pace yourself through a number of incremental asks:

- Incremental Ask 1: ask to meet (purpose: build rapport)
- Incremental Ask 2: ask for their willingness to use your app (purpose: obtain feedback)
- Incremental Ask 3: ask for their willingness to vouch for the product (purpose: obtain social proof)

Tip #18: Craft Emails that Get a Response

Whenever you are starting a venture, however big or small, you will need to reach out to other people for support of one form or another, whether it is for advice, contacts, funding, partnerships, collaboration, or technical guidance. Your predominant mode of communication will be through email. As such, emails have to be carefully crafted. Adhering to the following guidelines will maximize the likelihood of a response.

1. **Emails must be short.** No one likes to read long emails. Emails should be just one or two paragraphs long or no longer than 500 words, especially with initial emails. Briefly share what you're working on and how it might benefit the email recipient, and then request a call or a meeting. Raise no more than one key issue. If you have five great ideas, choose one. Save the others for future emails, so you will have four good reasons to follow up later!

2. **Make a personal connection.** Always refer to something specific about the recipient and give a clear reason for reaching out to that person in particular. Even if you have no genuine personal connection with the recipient, create one: by referring to a recent article about the recipient or the recipient's organization; by saying that someone (whom you need not name) suggested that you reach out to this person (for example, *"your name came up in a recent conversation and my mentor suggested that I reach out to you because..."*); or mentioning something that you and the recipient have in common, such as an alumni connection or industry involvement (for example, *"Hey Suzy, we noticed that you're an investor in Swirl. We are not competitors with Swirl, but given your understanding of the retail software, I would like to take half an hour to introduce you to our product...."*).

3. **State why you are reaching out.** For example, if you have had a prior relationship that has gone cold, don't pretend that you are reaching out to reconnect or to check in on the recipient. Be clear and honest about your reason for writing, which often will be to ask for a favor: *"I'm reaching out because..."* or *"I'm writing*

because..." Your recipients will appreciate your honesty, and they will often be glad to help.

4. **Make a specific ask**. Your email should conclude with a specific ask, which can be answered with a one word reply, such as "*Sure*" or "*OK*" or "*Absolutely!*" Do not conclude with a vague, open-ended question, such as "*That's my proposal, so what do you think?*" Instead, use a very specific question, such as "*I'd love to talk to you about it. Would it be okay if I reach out to your assistant to schedule a 15 minute phone conversation?*" Feel free to offer a less burdensome alternative as well. For example, you can say, "*It would be great if you have the time for coffee. Ultimately, I'm trying to get feedback on the pitch deck, but if email works best for you, that'd be appreciated, too.*" Your first email should usually conclude with a request for a phone call or a meeting. Do not ask for advice over email unless you have a pre-existing relationship.

5. **Limit the word "I"**. As you edit your email, emphasize the perspective and the concerns of the recipient. You should spend more time (more space) on the recipient's activities than on yourself and your own work. There will also be a balancing act between personalizing the message and showing there is more than one person behind the startup (*see Tip #8 on using the royal "we"*). Compare the following: your first draft might read, "*I created a new app and I think I know a way you could use it. I would love to talk to you about it sometime.*" Your final draft, however, might read, "*Our new HotShot app could save your organization millions of dollars with very little risk. Does this sound like something you would be interested in hearing more about?*"

6. **Personalize the subject line**. Reference a person, event, or product with which your recipient is familiar. "*Following up on...*" or "*Referred by...*" or simply "*our conversation*" are strong subject line phrases. "*Quick question*" or "*quick note*" are also excellent subject line phrases, since they immediately signal that the email will be short and direct. On the other hand, "*Hello*", "*Potential partnership*" and "*Meeting*" are clunky and dull and should be avoided in the subject line.

7. **Leverage the "college card."** Many people are eager to assist students, so don't be afraid to let people know of your student

status. For example, Nick Dougherty is the founder of VerbalCare, a company that created an iPad app that allowed stroke patients to communicate with their caregivers. To test his application in a clinical setting, he looked up which floor at a local hospital had the neurointensive care unit and contacted the head nurse. He told her he was a student at Boston University and was developing a technology to help stroke patients, and wanted to "pick her brain." She was very willing to support his school project, to let him shadow her and pilot his technology in the unit, and to recommend other relevant contacts for him.

8. **Chase unanswered emails.** Not everyone will respond to your first email. Do not interpret a lack of response as a rejection and give up on these unresponsive email recipients. Instead, send a follow up email. However, the follow up email should neither be a repeat of your first email nor a lengthy second message where you write about some other additional matter. Instead, you should hit reply to the email that your recipient has not yet responded to, and in one line, simply say *"Hi, I hope you are well. I just wanted to follow-up on the below email in case it was buried in your inbox. Many thanks."* This indicates that you are still waiting for a reply and offers a plausible excuse for why the recipient has not yet replied. This short reminder is usually effective in eliciting a response (and often a favorable one). (*See also Tip #58 about how to nudge a timely response.*)

The experiences of Michael Schmidt the founder of Vaska Technologies, a company that creates appliances that automate the replenishment of consumables, are instructive. In the early days of his startup, Michael would reach out to CEOs of consumer appliance companies. In his email, he would pose a series of questions about whether his idea had potential value to the company, in the hopes of cultivating a relationship and sparking interest in his technology. When that approach didn't work, Michael started requesting a short phone call to get feedback on a specific aspect of his startup or product, or to be directed to someone in the organization who would be able to provide feedback, rather than asking for written replies. Michael learned that busy CEOs are much more likely to grant a request for a short phone call (or to forward the message to an appropriate person) than to take the time to compose thoughtful responses in writing.

Writing short emails that open with a connection to the recipient and end with a direct ask that can easily be addressed with a "yes" or a "no" will maximize the positive responses to your outreach efforts. Now you can try to focus on making your asks as easy to say "yes" to as possible.

Tip #19: Make Easy Asks

Make it as easy as possible for people to say yes to you, not only in the sense of a one-word reply, but also in terms of what you ask for. Going back to our most recent example, Michael was on the right track. He had initially posed questions for CEOs to answer because he realized that he wasn't quite in the position to ask CEOs outright for a commitment to buy his technology. But he didn't realize that asking someone to compose a thoughtful response was equally onerous. Here are some ways to make "easy asks" that set the initial bar for involvement relatively low. Once you get someone involved, and when both parties have some familiarity and comfort with each other, you will find it easier to make bigger requests.

1. **Ask for small amounts of time**. Make a small initial request, and explicitly describe a minimally invasive time commitment. For example, rather than asking for a one-hour meeting, ask for fifteen minutes. Rather than asking someone to join your startup as a board member, ask if she would consider serving as an advisor for a six to twelve month period, with responsibilities limited to an occasional email or an hour phone call once a month.

2. **Ask for small levels of commitment**. Rather than asking for full-blown contracts, ask for letters of intent (or memoranda of understanding). These kinds of initial statements of commitment, without the full force of legally binding contracts, make it easier for parties to get involved with your startup. You can also leverage these initial statements of interest as forms of social proof, which in turn will encourage others to commit to your startup.

3. **Ask for recommendations**. If you ask people directly if they want to invest in a cause or take on a job, some of them will feel put on the spot and will hesitate to answer "yes." When you are recruiting someone for a position or to make a request, start with *"Do you know..."* and then describe the type of person, involvement, or assistance you are seeking. For example, when you are seeking an app developer and you are talking to an app developer, ask *"Do you know anyone who is looking for some part time work in app development?"* Or if you are seeking a board member and talking to someone who you want to join your board, ask *"Do you*

know anyone who has the time and interest to serve on a board?" In reality, you are hoping that the person you are talking to will want to take on the role. This low-key, non-threatening approach allows you to test the waters to see whether the person has an interest in getting involved, and even when the answer is "no", it can lead to other recommendations and contact information.

4. **Don't ask at all.** There are times when you do not want to make an overt ask because you feel it will put the other party in an uncomfortable position. Instead, simply state what you hope for (without insinuating that you expect the party to provide it) and describe how you are struggling to attain it. Your difficulty should be an impediment that the other party could easily fix or assist with a quick word or two. This allows you to make a subtle ask without putting someone on the spot. In short, you are sharing a difficulty and hoping someone who is in a position to help will volunteer assistance.

People want to help, but are afraid of overcommitting. Help them help you by making "easy asks" that require little time and commitment, and that don't put others on the spot.

Tip #20: Give Easy Outs

A corollary for making "easy asks" is giving "easy outs." Make it easy for people to turn you down in case they are not able or willing to help you. You might worry that you are imposing on others with your requests. But by offering easy outs, you can make your requests with more confidence and less discomfort. Even though you might want to make it hard for people to turn you down, making it as easy as possible saves face for everyone and preserves a relationship that might be useful to both parties in the future. Here are some ways to give easy outs:

1. **"Busy"**: Begin your request by saying, "I *know you must be so busy, but... [make your ask]*." Using the word "busy" signals that you are aware of the person's status or importance or existing commitments, and it builds in an excuse for the person to decline gracefully. And it might not just be an excuse. The person could genuinely like your idea but simply be too busy to get involved at the moment.

2. **"No worries."** Conclude your ask with an explicit out by saying "*No worries if you're not able to... [fulfill your ask]*." Telling someone that you are fine if they are not able to fulfill your request takes pressure off the person to do so. This allows you to preserve the relationship and to go back to the person at a later time, with a different ask.

3. **"Shift me."** Often initial requests are for a phone call or meeting. Even when you have successfully secured an upcoming scheduled phone call or meeting, you can add a line at the end of the email that the person should feel free to shift the scheduled call or meeting, if necessary. For example: "*Dear X, I'm so glad that you're willing to meet up despite your busy schedule. I look forward to seeing you on [date/time/location]. If your schedule changes, please don't hesitate to shift me.*" This message signals your respect, flexibility, and consideration and will make you a person that others want to work with in the future.

Each of these approaches follows a pattern: personal greeting, informing the person why you're writing, making the easy ask, giving an easy out, and expressing appreciation (as though the ask will be fulfilled). Messages that follow this pattern tend to elicit positive responses since most people do want to be helpful as long as doing so does not interfere with their other commitments. Doing all this to maximize positive responses will take you far, but even so, not everything will go as planned.

Tip #21: Prepare to Walk a Lonely Path

In your entrepreneurial journey, some people will join you at the beginning, others in the middle, and still others near the end. Some will stay with you all the way, while others will only be there for a portion of the way. In this sense, entrepreneurship is a lonely path. You will need to commit to walk this path alone, even as others come and go. You alone must be willing to shoulder this responsibility, to think several steps ahead, to keep focus on your central pillars, and to continually advance your startup with or without others. Your steadfast commitment, even when some abandon ship, will in fact inspire others to remain with you, or to join your effort.

Founders are optimistic people by nature. They have to think they can overcome the odds of startup failure and they may not have experienced personal or significant setbacks before. Those working on nonprofit startups may be particularly idealistic. But you need to prepare yourself:

1. **You will encounter feelings of self-doubt and lack of confidence.** While you are out there leveraging your contacts, asking for favors, pitching your idea, recruiting investors, board members, and advisors, and subjecting yourself and your vision to public scrutiny, you are going to feel vulnerable. You won't be sure if your idea is any good, if you are spending your time wisely, if you are chasing a pipe dream, or if you are even the right person to be spearheading the organization. You will also worry about imposing on other people's time and resources, and you won't be sure if others will buy into your idea. These doubts are natural and all founders feel them. Your challenge is to keep them at bay.

2. **You will lose relationships (and maybe a friend).** Just as in dating, not all of your relationships will survive. There is a good chance that at least one significant relationship, even possibly a longtime friendship, won't survive the upheavals and the pressures of startup life.

3. **People will disappoint you.** Even with extensive planning and preparation and the application of all the helpful ideas that you encounter, there will be times when you feel discouraged and let down. Here are some examples of how you may be disappointed:

- Someone will make a promise but not follow through.
- Someone will offer to connect you with a key contact or to invest in your enterprise and then back out or disappear.
- Someone will lie, cheat, or steal (yes, this happens!).
- Someone will act in self-interested or flagrantly selfish ways.
- Someone will say one thing and do another, acting without integrity.
- You also may be forced to take the blame even when you are not culpable, or watch others get credit they do not deserve.

4. **You hold ultimate responsibility.** The responsibility to run a startup can feel enormous. Founders who do gain traction often wonder if they are managing themselves, their teams, and their startup strategies in the best way possible. It is often the first time they have ever been truly responsible for others. For this reason, founders often want to work with co-founders. But even if you have a co-founder, you will still carry the burden and responsibility of the startup. As you delegate responsibilities, you cannot become complacent or overly dependent on others to advance the startup. If someone is not doing her job, you will need to find someone else to do it, or do it yourself. You must cultivate a proactive and assertive mindset: while others are waiting for an elevator, you are already climbing the stairs.

You will want to avoid disappointments as much as possible; despite your best efforts, disappointments will happen, and you should be ready to take things in stride when they do. No matter how honest you are in your dealings, how well you treat others, or how noble your cause, you will be hurt in the process of being an entrepreneur. Expect these disappointments to happen. As with any major creative project, there can be no birth without pain.

But take comfort in knowing that such pains are signals of your growth and progress. Remembering that entrepreneurship is a lonely process will strengthen your determination to move forward. But there may be another doubt in the back of your mind, a doubt about the worth of the project itself. Should you really carry on, or should you change course?

Tip #22: Pursue Productive Persistence

Many of the new founders interviewed emphasized the importance of persistence in keeping the startup alive, even when things do not seem promising. Occasionally we hear glamorous stories of founders who quickly raised venture capital, worked on their startup for a few years, and then sold their company and retired to an island. These stories, if true at all, are not representative of the experiences of most founders. Instead you'll most likely hear "no" a lot of times before you hear your first "yes."

Persistence entails a relentless pursuit of your startup goal even in the face of closed doors, obstacles, and rejections. For example, Omar Abudayyeh, a co-founder of Modalyst, described how difficult it was to obtain investor funding for an online marketplace. In meeting after meeting with potential investors, he was advised to come back when his team could demonstrate more revenue growth. Omar found this advice highly frustrating because Modalyst was seeking funding precisely to support the efforts that would make such growth possible. He felt discouraged by this ongoing chicken-or-egg situation, and he began to doubt whether his startup was a good idea. After two years of such meetings, however, his startup raised its seven figure seed round from angel investors. Persistence is an essential quality for any founder.

Be aware, however, that there are two kinds of persistence: unproductive and productive. **Unproductive persistence** consists of repeating the *same approach* over and over again, without any positive results, and expecting that as long as you keep at it, you will eventually succeed. The productive version involves constant experimentation with *new approaches* until you find one that really works. You will know that you are engaged in **productive persistence** when you are learning about what is or is not working. Productive persistence requires equal doses of determination and experimentation.

Now that you know approach others for assistance and involvement in your startup, you'll need to be selective about those you want to work with. The next chapter shares ideas of how to recruit a startup team, including co-founders and employees.

EINSTEIN SAYS:

Einstein said "Doing the same thing over and over and expecting a different result is insanity." Don't be insane. If you've been hitting your head against the wall for some time and have not been trying different strategies, stop. Instead, persistently experiment and try different, even unconventional, approaches.

PART FOUR

HOW TO RECRUIT A STARTUP TEAM

HOW TO RECRUIT A STARTUP TEAM

I'm looking to recruit a founding team for my startup. What's the best way to meet the right individuals? How do I get people interested in joining my venture? I also don't have much to pay someone.

No one can launch a big idea alone. While I didn't have a hard time recruiting team members (women and education are compelling causes that appeal to many people), I didn't know the right types of people to recruit or what to look for in potential founding team members, from co-founders to board members. When I did recruit individuals, it felt awkward to have early conversations about matters like titles, roles, responsibilities, and how decisions would be made in the event of disagreement. So we didn't. How was I supposed to bring up such touchy subjects when I felt so grateful to anyone willing to get involved with the startup? I hadn't learned then that such conversations are inevitably difficult, but absolutely necessary. In fact they are a first test of the startup's survival. I had acted like there were no stakes in this process – when there were. You too will be sacrificing time, money, and other opportunities, and risking personal relationships and assets. So there is a lot at stake and it will be important to find individuals who share your values and are equally committed to the startup and with whom you have a common understanding about how the startup will run. The tips below discuss how you can.

Tip #23: Gather Your Missing Puzzle Pieces

Running a startup means you'll need to know everything related to operating a small business. For example, most startups need attention to financing, legal obligations, technology, human resources, management, and fundraising. There are also areas more directly related to operations, including strategy, sales, and marketing. Even if you are talented in a lot of these areas, you won't be able to do everything.

Devote your time to the most essential functions of the startup and to the areas in which you are strongest. Meanwhile, recruit a team of people who are more capable than you in the other critical areas. You may not be able to hire or recruit your ideal candidates because they have options to work elsewhere, have limited time, and may be risk-averse. Nonetheless, there are strategies that you can use to recruit an effective team:

1. **Start with a current needs assessment of your startup**. Identify the skill sets that match the priorities of your startup at its particular stage. For example, in the beginning stages you may need more technical and fundraising skills. If you won't be reaching out to potential customers for another year, you may not need sales and marketing skills right away.

2. **Conduct a functional self-analysis of your own skills.** Once you identify what skills your startup needs at a given moment, you should conduct a functional self-analysis. Be brutally honest with yourself about the skills and areas of expertise that you do and do not possess. Your team should be built around your existing skills, interests, and talents. Given that it may be difficult to recognize your own shortcomings, ask advisors to give you their frank assessment.

3. **Recruit complementary rather than overlapping skills.** The more complementarity and the less overlap between the skills and resources on your team, the better for your enterprise. Overlapping skill sets may result in people stepping on each other's toes. While it is natural for us to want to work and spend time with others who are similar to ourselves, you will need to reach beyond your social comfort zone and recruit individuals who are explicitly different from yourself, in both personality and

expertise, but who complement the needs of the startup. If you are not an outgoing person and find it hard to start conversations or to pitch ideas easily, find someone with strong social and communication skills. If you lack technical skills, you must recruit someone with strong engineering or design ability. If you have a hard time staying organized, find someone to handle the small details so that you can work on bigger issues.

For example, Vienne Cheung, the founder of VienneMilano, wanted to start a company related to fashion. She had a degree in fine arts and business and a knack for fashion. At a networking event, she met an Italian man who had previously started an e-commerce company and was willing to invest in her business. When she shared that she liked Italian hosiery but couldn't find a good selection in the United States, he suggested a luxury hosiery line.

He was a good partner for Vienne because he knew Italian designers, had connections with manufacturers, and could supply the initial startup capital for the business. Vienne contributed her knowledge of fashion, design, and operations. She visited manufacturers, looked at samples, and chose the color, material, and design of the hosiery. She also handled the logistics of the startup by placing orders, overseeing payment and shipment, and developing the marketing and sales campaigns. She and her partner worked well together, and each contributed to different parts of the business. They made a great team.

In contrast, Lisa Walker, the founder of LearningInSync, did not assess her own skills or the needs of her startup before recruiting her team. As a result, she and her five co-founders enjoyed working with each other, but lacked complementary skill sets. While many of them were adept at design and could produce curriculum content and publication materials, none of them had much experience fundraising. While they could brainstorm fundraising ideas, none of them had the contacts, the professional networks, or the skills to raise money effectively. As a result, the startup folded after a year.

You might have both a great founding team and a great startup idea. However, if you can only have one of the two, a great founding team is more important than a great initial idea: a strong team can work together to fine-tune a mediocre startup idea and make it great, but without a strong team to start with, the idea and the startup have little chance to survive. As you build your team, investigate people's strengths, skills, and inclinations. Consider very carefully whether they bring something new and valuable to the team, and how well their qualities complement your skills and align with your startup's needs. Now that you know better who to look out for, how do you find them?

Tip #24: Cast a Wide Net

Whether you are looking for co-founders, partners, investors, board members, product test sites, advisors, employees, customers, or volunteers, you should connect with as many contacts as possible in order to assess their level of interest in your startup. You should be making contacts, pitching to a number of people, and growing your network.

1. **Proactively seek out relevant individuals to connect to.** Leverage your own social network, including your alumni network. You can also extend your search to incubators, accelerator programs, startup meetups, industry conferences, or career fairs. Pay special attention to their attendance or speakers lists – simply go online and search for startup meetups or startup accelerators in your city. You can also search websites such as Startuply at Crunchbase.com, AngelList.com, StartupHire.Com, or Stackoverflow.com, or post on Facebook startup groups.

    Consider investing in a premium LinkedIn account, since it allows you to search for individuals within a particular field and with specific job titles and to reach out to more people than with a regular account. Another proactive method is to search online for individuals who are writing or quoted in your startup space and to reach out to them. If you have the funds for it, consider utilizing recruiting firms, including those that specialize in skilled engineers from companies like High Tech Ventures. Finally, consider downloading Chrome extensions such as Newsle.com, FullContact.com, or Conspire.com, which allow you to obtain information on those with whom you are corresponding.

2. **Look for people who convey passion for the startup space that you are in.** Passionate team members drive and motivate productivity. Those who serve merely as "hired guns" will be less flexible and less committed to your startup. You can assess people's values by asking why they believe in the startup, what excites them about it, and why they want to be part of it. For example, Ann Chao, the founder of Sonation, Inc., a music technology company, attributes the success of her company to her recruitment of two app developers who were passionate about music. The app, called Pandanza, allows musicians to

play with a full orchestra that adapts to their playing. Although other developers told her it would take three to four developers and significant time to produce the technically complex app, she recruited two engineers who produced the app in just a few months. Even though they were in demand for other projects, they were highly motivated to work on the app, in part because they themselves were musicians and they were intrigued how the app was built from a musician's (rather than listener's) perspective.

3. **Keep your spout of contacts flowing.** Regardless of whether you win over any particular contact, you should end every call or meeting by asking, "*Is there anyone else I should talk to?*" This simple question keeps things moving and helps you to build a targeted list of contacts or investors who might be receptive to your startup idea. Since you won't know who all the players are, using one call or meeting to lead to the next ensures that you focus on the most relevant and promising contacts.

Once you have a good idea of the skills you need and how to connect with individuals with those skills, you'll need to ensure that you will actually work well together.

Tip #25: Find Chemistry

While it is essential to recruit a team with the right combination of skills, talents, connections, and experience, you will also need some basic chemistry with the people on your team. This doesn't mean you are looking for "yes" people. However, since you'll be spending a lot of time with your startup team and relying on them for success, you will want to find individuals who share your values, who are equally excited about the startup's mission and vision, and with whom you get along. When seeking team members that have chemistry, look for three distinct qualities: easy rapport, shared values, and work style.

1. **Easy rapport.** Do you feel at ease, and do you have open and natural communication with the person? Would you feel comfortable sitting next to this person for several hours on an airplane? First impressions count a lot when assessing rapport. Also consider whether this person will have good rapport with others on your team. For example, a very aggressive person who overshadows others and consumes a lot of attention and energy will probably not be a good fit, regardless of her particular skills, talents, or experience.

2. **Shared values.** Does this person share your underlying values and believe in the purpose and mission of the startup? Your best performers will be those who are truly inspired by the startup's mission (what is being done) and vision (why it's being done).

3. **Similar work styles.** How do people manage their work and time? How do they teach and learn, interact with others, contribute to the team, and communicate? Someone who is serious, hardworking, and wants to tackle problems is not a good fit for a work culture where others are more casual about their work and timelines.

    To understand how someone works, investigate whether she prefers to work independently or collaboratively, whether she prefers administrative tasks or tasks that require initiative, whether she is more innovative or more traditional, whether she tends to be highly communicative and collaborative or more reserved and independent, whether she respects hierarchy greatly or view most individuals as equals, and how she handles setbacks and stress. Also look for whether a person falls into a particular work style model, such as: ensuring that lists are checked, building relationships and ensuring consensus, or researching and understanding problems in a deliberate and disciplined way.

If you've built a good team, you will all be working hard and still having fun together. Once you have built a team with whom you have good chemistry, make sure you agree on a decision-making culture. To avoid debating issues ad nauseam, carve out roles and responsibilities and include this as part of your explicit work culture. (*See also Tip #68 on expecting conflict.*)

As you go about recruiting a startup team, you'll also need to consider which individuals should be elevated to or granted co-founder status.

Tip #26: Recruit Co-Founders

A co-founder is not a technical or legal term: it is an honorific title (such as calling someone your boyfriend or girlfriend) that recognizes someone's significant trustworthiness, involvement, commitment, and contribution to the startup during the ideation or early stages of the enterprise. Granting someone co-founder status often also means granting an equity stake (not so with nonprofits). Before inviting someone to join your startup efforts as a co-founder, heed the below advice:

1. **Accomplish as much as you can before having to give away co-founder status or an equity stake.** There are three general circumstances in which someone becomes a co-founder: (i) when a founder has an idea and doesn't do much work on it and finds other like-minded individuals to work on the idea together; (ii) when two individuals brainstorm an idea and begin working on it together; and (iii) when a founder works alone, gains traction and needs additional assistance, but cannot afford to hire the help needed.

   In the latter case, before turning team members or startup supporters, such as advisors, into co-founders, and before giving away an equity stake (or board membership, the equivalent of an equity stake in the nonprofit context), do absolutely as much as you can before having to give away this high stakes prize. The more traction and momentum you have gained before you recruit this way, the more claim you will have to a superior equity stake for yourself.

2. **Make sure to test for initial commitment and contribution.** Any kind of co-founder title, equity ownership, or board membership that you give away must be earned. For example, Shantanu Guar co-founded Allurion Technologies with his medical school classmate. Allurion builds gastric balloons that can be ingested so individuals can shrink their stomach volume and combat obesity without needing surgery. They invited two people to become equal partners in the company only after they demonstrated their commitment and contribution to the startup. One new partner brought financial expertise and strategic thinking, was willing to move from a part-time role to a full-time CEO role, and made a

small investment in the company. The other new partner was a physician and a gastro-endocrinologist with both clinical expertise and experience developing medical devices for the gastrointestinal tract. He also was well-connected to a large network of investors in the medical space, and had helped raise the first seed round of funding. As Shantanu said, *"They earned their keep."*

3. **Start the conversation by asking promising candidates if they you want to get more involved.** Kyle Kahveci is the founder of Advanced Continuing Education Association (ACEA), a software program that tracks continuing education credits for professionals in different industries. He was looking for potential co-founders, especially those with a technical background. He ended up hiring two freelance developers part-time at a reasonable market rate. He did not initially mention co-founding or equity, but after some time he saw that they worked effectively together and wanted to recruit them as co-founders. To do so, he reviewed with them the significant progress they had accomplished together over the past three months, and asked how they felt about their experience working together.

    Since they had a similarly positive experience, he asked: *"Do you want to get more involved?"* Use these words to ask if someone would like to step up her involvement, responsibilities, and expectations to the level of co-founder (or full-time employee or board member). You will be able to hear what circumstances might impact someone's commitment and contribution levels before formally inviting her on as a co-founder, and you avoid putting anyone on the spot.

4. **Once you decide to work with someone else as a co-founder, distinguish between giving away (a) co-founder title, (b) equity ownership, and (c) board membership.** New founders often confuse these and assume that offering up one means offering up the other. However, each of these negotiable items is valuable in its own right. For example, one can have an equity stake and have even joined the company early, but not be granted the "co-founder" title. One can also have a co-founder title, but not be granted equal equity. Similarly, one can be a board member without having equity or a co-founder title. Consider each of these positions and titles a distinct "resource" that you can trade away. Consider carefully when and to whom you might want to do so.

5. **Once you recognize someone as a co-founder, prepare to talk through difficult issues**. Each founder's agreement is unique, but forming *some* sort of agreement has value. The key issues you'll need to discuss include: role and responsibilities, ownership, decision-making, and expected contributions. This discussion may be very uncomfortable, but it is a process that all founders go through. (See also Noam Wasserman's *Founder's Dilemma*). For example, ask questions, such as:

   - Who gets what percentage of the business? Why?
   - What are the roles and responsibilities of the founders?
   - Is there a pecking order or hierarchy and what does it look like?
   - What financial or in-kind contributions should founders invest in the startup?
   - How are salaries determined for founders and how do they change?
   - How are decisions made? (majority vote, unanimous vote, or CEO)
   - What happens when one founder isn't living up to expectations or departs?
   - What will the co-founders' relationship be with other parties, such as the board, investors, clients, or customers?
   - What is the overall goal and vision for the startup?

6. **Dividing up equity will likely be the most difficult topic of conversation.** When do you give it, how much, to whom, and based on what criteria? Importantly, determinations of equity ownership stakes are **subjective and negotiated.**

   - *Seek outside help.* There is no magic number, and you should consult outside help (such as legal counsel, potential investors, startup advisors), as they may provide experience or (if you are already working with other co-founders) an unbiased view that the entire team can trust. Do your own research as well, and check out sites like Foundrs.com that provides a "co-founder equity calculator."
   - *Agree on principles.* Most people want to be compensated on "fair" terms but what is fair is very subjective. Splitting equity

evenly may be the best answer, but don't land there by default. Instead, agree on the relevant factors, assign each of these items a weight (for example, 10% or 20% of the total), and allocate equity based on each partner's contribution. Some principles or factors you should consider are:

- origination of the idea
- capital investments (usually trumps other considerations)
- sweat equity (prior work and critical role)
- sacrifices made (forgone salaries, job or other opportunities)
- risks assumed
- time commitment
- industry or startup experience
- role expertise or seniority
- key connections
- intellectual property
- expectations of future roles, time commitment (e.g., full-time or part-time) and financial contributions

- *Be unemotional. Stick to the reasons.* Co-founders are often personally connected – either by friendship, family, or previous work experience. This can make it especially difficult to split equity, as you don't want to hurt feelings or burn bridges. Work hard not to let emotions dictate equity-splitting decisions, and stick to reasons and principles as much as you can.

- *Agree to revisit equity arrangements.* If there are uncertainties that need to be resolved, establish principles for an equity arrangement and agree to split only when larger uncertainties are resolved. If you and your potential partners can't get through this discussion in a timely fashion and come to agreement, then it's unlikely that your startup can ultimately survive anyway.

- *Vest all shares (whether for co-founders or employees).* Finally, regardless of how the equity is divided, all shares should be subjected to vesting restrictions where equity owners are allocated a block number (not a percentage) of shares and earn a portion of those shares only for each year of work ("earn as you go"). For example, co-founders may earn their equity allocation over a period of 4 years with a 1-year cliff. If they leave before the first year, they get nothing; after one year, two years, or three years, they get 25% of the allocation; and after four years, they get the full 100%. While you may not see this as an issue now, you never know what a co-founder will do in six months or a year.

With these tips to get the best co-founders and other titled personnel, you can clear many of the hurdles you'll encounter as your startup grows. Be aware also that your team members may not all come from the same walks of life. You might find it useful to look for co-founders in a younger cohort or your peers.

4CS OF DIAMOND CO-FOUNDERS:

The best co-founders are like diamonds and exhibit the 4Cs:

- Chemistry (you get along)
- Complementarity (few duplicative skills)
- Commitment (both care equally)
- Contribution (both materially advance the startup)

Tip #27: Don't Overlook the Little People

In casting a wide net (*see Tip #24*), don't assume that only older, well-established, and wealthy individuals have the resources to help you. Startups are made with sweat, and you'll need worker bees to help lift your startup off the ground. People who are older and more established are unlikely to do that heavy lifting for you unless they have a financial interest in your company or are paid employees. Young people, however, have the time and energy that you need. They are creative problem solvers and will experiment with new approaches. They also have the resiliency to pick themselves up and keep going, even if they fail at some task (at first).

So take a careful look at your own peers! Email your friends, and leverage the social network of your siblings' or friends' peer groups. College and graduate students are often looking for ways to gain experience and to work on something they are passionate about. Pitch your idea to them, and seek out their involvement in your startup:

- **Post internship opportunities** at local colleges or universities with the career office or specific departments (e.g., the computer science department if you're looking for coders or the art studio department if you're looking for artists, etc.).

- **Look for college clubs or classes** that relate to your startup. The president of the club or the professor of the class may be willing to share your startup opportunity.

- **Connect with young professionals** who are often looking for exciting projects outside of work. Professional associations or the pro bono contacts at corporate firms are a good starting point.

- **Become an employer-partner** for required work experience programs at colleges and universities. For example, Desmond Lim, the founder of Quikforce, an online platform to book appointments with moving companies, tapped into Northeastern's Co-op Program, where he was able to obtain coders who needed to fulfill their internship requirement.

In my own startup, the Asian Women's Leadership University Project, I saw how instrumental young people were achieving the startup's various milestones. For example, Smith College students expressed enthusiasm for the project, which encouraged the college president to pitch institutional support of the project to the board of trustees, which led Smith College to become an academic planning partner for the new university. Other Smith students studying abroad at the London School of Economics nominated the AWLU Project to present at the TEDx conference at LSE, which gave us publicity and exposure. In addition, another young Smith alumna who was a freelance journalist wrote an article that was published in the New York Times. Board members did not secure such high visibility opportunities for the organization, but current and recent college students did.

Help can come from unexpected places, and young people can be great catalysts for your startup. They can also be your best resource when money is tight.

Tip #28: Money Isn't Everything

Although you may be a cash-strapped startup and you may not be able to pay for all the help you need, don't think that all you have to offer is money or that individuals are only interested in financial gain. There are many things that you can offer that aren't financial.

For example, even if you are not able to offer top market salaries, you may offer employees and volunteers:

- an opportunity to develop new skill sets
- an opportunity to build a portfolio of work
- an opportunity to receive strong references when they move to their next role
- mentorship opportunities
- resume, startup, or professional experiences
- a resume gap filler when someone is in between jobs
- the freedom to craft their own schedules or to work with initiative

Other intangibles you may offer to those who may not receive a financial stake include:

- a title, board membership, or organizational affiliation
- satisfaction from mentoring a young person
- a way to demonstrate a commitment to important values
- a sense of belonging to a community
- a sense of purpose or mission (especially for retirees)
- an opportunity to be part of a journey or an exciting venture
- opportunities to learn
- an expanded social circle
- your sincere appreciation

Rayfil Wong is the founder of ProfessorSavings, an ad-based revenue business that teaches basic financial literacy on video. He often needs to hire talented freelancers to develop instructional videos, but is on a tight budget. To attract and retain his freelancers, he lets them know that their salary does not indicate how he values them, but represents his budgetary constraints. As he says, "*I make sure to tell my freelancers that they are worth more than I could ever pay, but that I value their willingness to work with me and that as the company and the number of projects grow, I will be loyal in rehiring them for future projects. I also give assurances that I will make efforts to give them new projects that expand their work portfolio, professional experience, and circle of contacts, things that they can carry into their next career moves.*"

Your having someone's interests in mind and being willing to assist that person in the future are powerful incentives, especially for a young prospect. As Rayfil said, "*I can't offer a salary at the level that people deserve all the time, but I can help get people where they need to go.*" Entrepreneurs know that looking out for someone's best interests is a skill.

As an entrepreneur, you have to believe that you are full of resources and have a lot to give. Knowing what you can offer to a prospective volunteer or employee will take you a long way toward finding and recruiting the people you need.

Tip #29: Recruit Based on Your Startup Stage

There are three common hiring stages of a startup: initial, ramp up, and steady. When you have a founding team in place and are recruiting volunteers or employees, you should determine which hiring stage you are at so that your hiring strategy reflects your needs.

1. **At the initial stage, onboard new hires or team members quickly, because you do not yet have a track record of success, nor can you offer the job security, salary levels, or the brand of an established company.**

   - *Filter out the clearly bad candidates and hire the best of the remaining candidates for a trial period.* Don't agonize over new hires at the beginning. You'll need to move fast and take whoever you can get. Interviews don't tell you much about how well a person will perform in a startup environment. A trial period, a single project or a three-month internship, however, allows you and your employee to feel each other out. It will you give a good sense of whether the individual is a long-term fit for your startup.

   - *Give responsibility and watch.* Look for those who consistently deliver on simple commitments in a timely fashion. Give more challenging projects to those who seem dependable, and continue to assess their skills and their ability to attract talented new hires. Even if you are looking for a specific technical skill set, note well which employees are well rounded, flexible, and capable of working cross-functionally, since they are most valuable during the lean years of a startup.

   - *Throughout your startup effort, always assess who commits and contributes most.* Commitment is emotional connection to the startup and the devotion of personal energy. Contributions are concrete efforts, such as product development, marketing, fundraising, or some other key action that materially advance the startup. These two qualities define the most productive and passionate members of your startup, those who will become your best lieutenants.

2. **In the ramp up stage, hire the most experienced person you can find, since at this stage you will know exactly how each new employee contributes directly to measurable goals:**

    - *Outline your ideal candidate profile and find the best person for the role.* Consider the specific role and task you expect the new hire to take on, the experience and level of specialization the new hire should have, the salary range you plan to offer, the type of career ambition the new hire should have, and who in your existing team the new hire will need to work well with. Someone who has "CEO" stamped on her forehead is not going to be happy in a role where creativity is not needed.

      Hire the person who best meets the profile you have drawn up. For example, Ben Jabbawy is the founder of Privy.com, a company that offers technology to analyze how social media campaigns lead to in-store revenue. Once the technology was sufficiently developed and Ben was able to raise some capital, he sought to hire an experienced sales manager. He ended up recruiting a former vice-president of sales at Microsoft who had scaled a small team up to twenty people and whose team had generated a couple million dollars in revenue.

    - *Focus primarily on work performance.* In the initial stage you'll largely take whoever you can get and reward loyalty, since recruiting will be difficult; in the ramp up stage, not only will you be in a better position to hire, but work performance will become a key criterion. As Sara Gragnolati, the founder of Cocomama Foods, a company that produces gluten-free food products, says, *"In the early stage of my company, I prioritized trust, relationships, and loyalty, since it's always a challenge to recruit as a startup. I gave people a longer leash. Now, as a funded company, I value performance over loyalty."*

    - *Ensure that everyone in your startup interviews the new hire.* Since the startup will still be relatively small at this stage, different functional teams will still need to talk to and work with each other, so it's important to make sure that the new hire gets along even with those outside of the new hire's functional role.

3. **In the steady stage, missing a role doesn't stall operations, and you have less anxiety about making the type of hire that your**

startup needs. If you get to this stage, congratulations! You are no longer a startup, but a business.

Now that you know what you want when hiring at different stages, you can grab the people who have the most to offer you. However, some very talented people will still not be good fits. But how can you tell?

Tip #30: Notice Bad Hires

Although you will work hard to make the best hires you can, not everyone you hire will end up being a perfect fit for your startup. Interviews don't tell you much about how newcomers will deal with a fast-moving and quickly evolving organization, where there may be little structure or stability. New founders also will rarely have much experience making hiring decisions and evaluating individuals' performance. Here are the qualities that indicate a bad hire:

1. **Weak performance**. In a startup, it can be difficult to determine whether someone's work performance is weak or whether the task is simply difficult. You can distinguish between the two, however. If you discuss your expectations, but continually find yourself offering strategies that someone should be generating on her own or if you're not getting the execution you want, switch that person out. The next random hire will probably leave your startup no worse off.

2. **Inflexibility**. Someone who has a bad attitude, insists on doing things her way, or says a task is out of her work scope will not be a reliable member of your startup. A startup is a constantly evolving entity and will need the flexibility to move in different directions. New or different skills will be needed all the time. If someone prefers to do only a certain type of work, disagrees with the new approach, or lacks the skill sets that are needed to carry out a new role – in other words, if the person cannot adapt to changing needs, switch her out for someone new.

3. **Bad culture fit**. If someone is too aggressive, passive or pessimistic, or complains about things that no one else is complaining about, she may cause unease in the organization. *Even if someone is highly productive*, she will sap your startup's energy and morale and make it more likely that the other members of your startup will leave or greatly reduce their productivity. It won't be worth it to keep one such member at the expense of the others.

4. **Desire for change without understanding.** New hires who enthusiastically identify how they want to immediately change the startup or who offer unsolicited suggestions during the interview

stage – without first trying to understand the organization – are a red flag. A startup is hard enough to run without someone who, knowingly or not, wants to hijack it.

5. **Lack of respect**. Many new founders have never yet met employees who act unprofessionally and may not know what behavior to tolerate. You need to have some bright lines: if an employee acts unprofessionally – playing a computer game during a client meeting, swearing at you, or doing anything that appears unethical or dishonest – that person needs to be removed immediately. Rehabilitating this person is not your job and not worth your time.

Whatever your filters are in the hiring stage, you won't catch every bad apple. Sometimes you'll have to let people go and that is a skill in itself.

Tip #31: Be Prepared to Fire People

Firing individuals is a difficult process. A new founder has usually never fired anyone – certainly never someone that she hired. Most startups, however, will wind up with at least one hire who is not a good fit for the organization. This isn't necessarily the fault of the startup or the founder or a mark of poor leadership. It is just part of the process of founding and running an organization. If you have raised your concerns with the employee and haven't noticed any satisfactory changes, or if you can't find a role that would be a better fit, it is time to part ways. Here are some strategies to deal with an employee who you need to let go:

1. **Implement performance reviews.** Regular performance reviews or project debrief sessions allow you to convey honest and specific feedback to your employees and to put individuals on notice or on probation (and it is best to establish these protocols before taking employees on). Explain to new hires that such reviews benefit the employee, as well as the company. For example, the employee will have the opportunity to give the company feedback and enhance their own professional development. To ensure that reviews feel fair and professional, develop clear guidelines and criteria.

2. **Transition someone quickly (or slowly when required).** Let people go early rather than giving third and fourth chances or waiting several months once it is clear that the situation is not improving. You don't want to expend additional effort managing that person or delay onboarding someone else. "Transition" is a good euphemism for "firing" or "removing" or "letting someone go."

    In some instances you'll need to transition the person slowly because work processes depend on this person or the person holds valuable information or relationships. To transition the person slowly, find a replacement or draw up a tentative plan for how to delegate the workload, and begin to scale back the person's work responsibilities. In all instances, remain respectful and professional at all times. In most cases, the individuals you let go will make positive contributions in another organization.

3. **Don't get into the details.** To transition a person quickly, call her into the office and privately and respectfully let her go by saying something short and succinct. Don't say someone did a good job. Simply use a positive adjective. For example, say, *"You are smart, but this isn't the right fit."* This is the compassionate path, and it allows the person to leave a position that did not offer her a future (or probably provide much satisfaction). You can offer to write a recommendation letter, to be in touch in the future, or to mentor the person, if you are so willing. But don't get into the details of what the person did wrong or how she fell short.

Senthil Balasubramanian, the founder of Sistine Solar, a company that produces aesthetic coverings for solar panels, needed to transition an employee. He remembered from business school that he was supposed to keep the conversation short and to avoid details because of the possible legal ramifications. Yet he thought the employee deserved to know why the company was letting her go. Giving a reason felt like the "right way" to treat an employee. However, when he explained how he liked some aspects of her work but not others, she challenged his decision and said, "You said I'm doing a lot of good work but you are still letting me go. I'm hearing you say that I am top caliber but that it's still not working out."

Unfortunately, he learned that despite his good intentions, it was better not to get into the details. The person being fired can deduce your reasons, especially if you've provided specific feedback earlier on. If the individual still wants to talk further, have her call you in a few weeks. That way you can separate the firing from any feedback.

Once you have a core startup team that you can work with, you will need to build a larger support network comprised of advisors and board members. The next chapter offers suggestions of how to identify and recruit such individuals to your startup.

PART FIVE

HOW TO RECRUIT ADVISORS AND BOARD MEMBERS

HOW TO RECRUIT ADVISORS AND BOARD MEMBERS

I want to tap the wisdom, experience, and help of advisors and board members. How do I convince busy executives or industry leaders to assist my startup in an official capacity? Are there guidelines on how I should best build my board or set of advisors?

Although I was able to find young college students and professionals to assist with my startup, I also wanted to find individuals with more authority and experience to join the AWLU Project. But I didn't know who would make a good advisor or the best way to approach individuals to join an advisory council. In addition, to formalize our activities and incorporate as a 501(c)(3) nonprofit organization, we would need to establish a board. But I had never built a board before and didn't know what factors to consider when building one. What types of people were the *right* types? What should I expect from their board service? You may find yourself in a similar situation, unsure how to approach someone whom you want to recruit as an advisor or board member. You may not even be sure what an advisory council or board is for. This chapter's tips, however, give guidance on how to cultivate relationships with, and what to look for in, potential advisors and board members.

∞◆∞

Tip #32: Dribble, Don't Drown People with Information

Many new, young founders, in their enthusiasm to demonstrate the merits of their startup, send lengthy emails that describe the big idea, tout the achievements made thus far, and include multiple attachments such as reports, business plans, or dense PowerPoint slides.

While you might think that you are being efficient by making information easily available, you can easily overwhelm the recipient with too much information too soon. The recipient might feel pressured by such an exhaustive and exhausting email. People can only handle so much information at one time. Contain your enthusiasm and limit the information you send to what is most relevant to that particular conversation.

1. **You want to share enough information to convey what your startup is about, but not every last detail.** Have patience and share information a little at a time. At the early stages of a relationship, the person you are messaging is not yet thinking about collaborating, partnering, joining, or investing in your startup. The purpose of your initial contact is to peak interest and establish some rapport only.

2. **If the first interaction goes well, then ask for permission to share additional information.** Feel free to indicate how the information might be of interest or beneficial to the other party. For example, you can say in an email or at the end of a meeting: *"Hi Sherry, great talking to you. As mentioned, we've produced a report that talks about the growth potential of the product. We'd be happy to share it, if you'd like. It might give you a better perspective on the opportunities the industry is identifying."*

Give people the space to choose how much they want to be informed and involved. People tend to regard information as more valuable when they have requested it than when it has been given away freely. Dribbling out information a bit at a time also allows you to measure the degree of interest in your startup and to determine the aspects of your startup that others find most compelling. As you go along, you can show them you really have the good stuff.

DRIBBLE NOT DROWN:

New founders in their enthusiasm often confuse the mantra of "share widely" with "share everything." Mistake! Individuals can only handle so much information at any one time. Share only information that is relevant to that particular communication to avoid drowning others in details they may not be ready to hear.

Tip #33: Show that You are an Insider

When you do connect with a key contact, show that you belong in the industry space by demonstrating that you know the key players, key companies or organizations, industry terminology, and industry publications. You will need to do your homework. Talk with any friends who work in the industry. Read up on the industry, check the news for relevant articles and events, Google search your contacts, learn about their work and about the mission of their organizations and other organizations in the same space. **Reference your industry knowledge** when you are meeting contacts and as you talk about your startup.

Demonstrating that you are an insider will make a real difference with recruiting potential advisors or board members, with fundraising, with potential partnerships, and even with supplier relationships. For example, when talking with prospective manufacturers, you might ask, "*How much does it cost to produce 1000 widgets?*" But if you learned their lingo, you might start asking, "*What is your minimum order quantity?*" When you use this industry terminology, manufacturers will be more likely to forgo other production opportunities and take your order, because they view you as a serious client. In short, people trust insiders. They will open up to you and take you more seriously if you talk like one.

When new contacts start referring you to people you already know, you've infiltrated the industry circle! Once you have, it will be a good basis from which to build more deep relationships with key contacts.

Tip #34: Cultivate Relationships

New founders are always asking about "how to pitch" or "how to raise money." They assume that there's a certain turn of phrase – rather than a crucial *process* – that will clinch a commitment. However, you must build trust and relationships before you make a substantial request of anyone. Would you propose marriage on the first date? Or accept such a proposal? Probably not. Similarly, do not expect people to make any investment or substantial commitment in your enterprise based on an initial conversation or meeting. They don't know enough about you or your startup yet to decide. Instead, **date first, then marry**.

When seeking the long-term, substantial involvement or investment of a potential partner, you will need to go through a process of cultivation. This means engaging, maintaining contact, and building trust and familiarity. The cultivation process is crucial to exploring the potential fit between you and the other party. To cultivate relationships:

1. **Connect on a personal level.** Do your homework before any meeting so you can connect on a personal level before launching into a business conversation. Read up on where your counterparts went to college, what businesses or organizations they are associated with, and what new developments have happened at their company. When you walk into a room, you should be knowledgeable about whomever you are meeting and prepared to connect.

2. **Ask contacts about their work or past experiences.** New founders often launch into a conversation about their startup. After all, that's the purpose of the meeting. However, you need to engage with people on matters that are important to them first, before delving into your own work. Ask about your contacts' interests or current or past projects, find out what they care about, and ask about their own experience in the industry. By seeking their opinions on matters of mutual interest, you will learn about their values, agendas and motivations, and about how you might work together. This engagement will allow you to get to know each other better and to assess whether you share mutual and aligned interests.

   For example, Lindsay Hyde, the founder of Strong Girls, Strong Women, a nonprofit organization that provides a mentoring program for young women, attributes her success to visiting communities with a sense of inquiry. Rather than imposing a mentorship model for girls in a given place, she would host a conference and bring together all the organizations serving girls in that area and ask about current resources and mentorship opportunities for them, inquire about any gaps existing in those services and programs, and investigate who could best fill that gap. Sometimes, she found that her mentorship program was not necessary, because there were already several mentorship programs running. However, by building relationships and reaching out and asking many questions, she and her organization could be highly effective when they did open up a mentorship program in a particular area.

3. **Ask for advice (and share how you have followed it).** Asking people for their advice implies that you respect their expertise and experience. Importantly, demonstrate that you value their feedback by following up on the advice and suggestions that they share. When you have done so, reach out again with an update (and a thank you). People will feel honored that you respected their opinion, and they will feel proud that their ideas helped you out. When they see you taking their advice seriously, they will become more and more invested in your enterprise.

4. **Share updates and relevant articles.** A quick email sharing good news about your startup's progress keeps your contacts connected to your efforts. Sharing news relevant to their work is also a way to show that you are thinking of them, their business, and their projects. Keep a regular schedule for your updates, such as a monthly email.

5. **Finally, notice which relationships are "sprouting."** Contacts who respond to your messages with suggestions, encouragement, or congratulations are signaling their willingness to become further involved in your enterprise. Once you have identified your sprouting contacts, you can prepare to make a request or to present a proposal that will more deeply engage them in your startup, such as official advisors or board members.

PRO TIP:

People are more likely to invest in your projects when their ideas have been incorporated. Add the word "DRAFT" to the top of proposals to signal that there is room for input and modification.

With your new relationships, make sure you act as a proper gardener and cultivate the new growth – and nothing encourages growth more than success.

Tip #35: Celebrate Little Successes

Convincing others that your vision is worthwhile and then earning their confidence that you have what it takes to achieve it are among your most important responsibilities as a founder. Publicizing and celebrating small victories as they occur will reveal the progress that your startup is making and convince others that your startup is a winning team.

1. **Label any small progress that your startup has made a success, and periodically share small successes with your contacts.** Notice the phrase "small successes." This phrase emphasizes the importance of scaling down the level of achievement needed to inspire confidence in your leadership and in your startup's potential.

2. **Establish a pattern of accomplishment.** A *pattern* of consistent but modest accomplishment is more impressive than a single major achievement followed by months of silence. A pattern of accomplishment is particularly critical because it creates a model for how you will achieve your most ambitious goals. For example, you might have the goal of raising millions of dollars for your enterprise. As the founder, you need to instill in others the confidence that this achievement is within the realm of possibility.

    Emphasize to your team that a record of little victories and a pattern of modest ongoing progress represent the true path to success. When people see that path, their confidence in the startup and in you will rise. Examples of small successes that relate to the goal of fundraising include: identifying a potential major investor who might be receptive to your startup, finding a connection to that investor within your network, obtaining the contact information of that investor, crafting and sending out an email to the investor, and getting a response. Consider each one of these steps an independent success, and celebrate each one as such. Even a *negative response* can be celebrated as a success of sorts, because it provides information about which avenues and networks you should and should not pursue.

3. **Name the individuals who have helped achieve each success and tell them that without their contribution, effort, or idea,**

you couldn't have done it. Recognize progress and give credit to those who made it possible in private conversations, in circulated internal and external newsletters, and at meetings. You can say something like, "*Mary had the great idea that inspired the startup to pursue [a course of action]. This strategy allowed us to increase our number of users fourfold.*" You want to signal that other people are contributing important ideas. Attribute successes to investors, advisors, employees, board members, volunteers, and so on, so they will continue to contribute in positive and proactive ways. If you make someone look good, they inevitably want to work hard for you and make you look good, too.

As you strive to reach your Big Goal, focus on the small successes that inspire motivation and support. As you report these successes, step back and observe how people respond to your periodic reports. Those who respond positively and encouragingly will, over time, become your strongest supporters. But how can you cement their support?

Tip #36: Build Stakeholder Interest

A stakeholder is anyone who is committed to your project and who stands to substantially contribute to the startup. Every contact is a potential stakeholder, and in order to transform a contact into stakeholder, you must demonstrate how the contact will benefit in some way from her involvement in your project. (*See also Tip #64 about the need to consider your audience and being mindful of "what's in it for them."*) A stakeholder can even be an organization whose support, involvement or contract you need. Here are some suggestions on how to build stakeholder interest and secure enduring forms of support:

1. **Figure out who need to become your stakeholders.** Promising stakeholders have both the *willingness and ability* to contribute substantially to your startup, whether it is capital, technical know-how, high-level connections, industry expertise, or some other valuable resource. (*See also Tip #23 on conducting a needs assessment for your startup.*) Stakeholders can provide a long-term contract, or become a major investor, a critical employee, or a well-connected board member. Be deliberate about your choices, since it will take a significant and personal investment of time and energy to cultivate a stakeholder's interest.

2. **Stakeholders' interests need not be financial.** They can be anything that a stakeholder finds valuable. (*See also Tip #34 on cultivating a relationship with key partners or potential partners.*) Explicitly ask yourself these three questions:

   - What do they get out of involvement with the startup right now?
   - What can they get out of it in the future?
   - How can I help them get something out of it?

3. **Plant the seeds of interest by communicating how your startup may benefit stakeholders.** Once you know who your stakeholders are, what they are interested in and would find valuable, allude to these benefits (or even mention them directly, if appropriate). You can talk about beneficial outcomes, even if those outcomes haven't materialized yet. By "planting seeds" about these potential outcomes, you spark their imagination.

4.   **Even do-gooders and altruistic supporters should have a stakeholder interest.** Most people are self-interested to some degree, even do-gooders. This is not a bad thing. It just means that people whose values and interests are best aligned with your project are those most likely to prioritize it. Similarly, social welfare organizations both have altruistic purposes and specific interests and motivations that you should take into account. Don't assume, for example, that a philanthropic organization committed to something as broad as children's health doesn't have its own concrete objectives or agenda. No matter how altruistic your potential stakeholder, work to identify how your startup, in particular, meets that stakeholder's interests.

5.   **All stakeholders' success should be tied to your success.** This means that if your startup succeeds, stakeholders stand to benefit in some way. This connection helps you build a solid base of support, motivates and inspires others to become greater contributors to your enterprise, and invests others in the success of the startup.

Remember, stakeholders may not be financial investors, but they are invested in other ways. Search out stakeholders who can offer all types of capital, from money to advice. The latter may contribute immeasurably to the success of your venture.

Tip #37: Recruit Advisors

Advisors are a great way to inject your startup with experience, wisdom, and connections. They also add social proof since the involvement of people with experience and cachet lends credibility to your venture. (*See Tip #9 about obtaining social proof for your organization.*) Some advisors may even become future board members or investors. Here are some suggestions on how to obtain advisors for your startup:

1. **Start with informal advising**. Do not immediately ask someone to serve as an advisor. Rather, seek out informal advice first. At the conclusion of a good conversation, ask if you can reach out again. If the person provides helpful advice a few times in a row and is willing to be available to you, then invite this person to become a formal advisor. Do this by email rather than on the phone, to avoid putting people on the spot. (*See Tip #34 about cultivating relationships before making significant asks for time or commitments from others. See also Tip #17 about pacing your asks.*)

2. **Describe areas where you need help or guidance**. When you approach someone to become an advisor, leverage your inexperience to increase the likelihood that the person will agree to advise you. Also describe why you would value the potential advisor's involvement in the startup.

    For example, Omar Abudayyeh, the co-founder of Modalyst, initially would reach out and say that he was working on a new revolutionary e-commerce site, had accomplished several significant milestones, and had been featured in various publications. Then he would ask if the contact would be willing to advise his new startup. He thought this approach would make it attractive for a potential advisor to assist his company, but few people agreed. When Omar changed his approach to include sharing the areas where he was struggling and how much he valued the opportunity to learn, he got many more positive responses.

    Most individuals want to help and share their expertise, and they especially enjoy giving mentorship to the younger generation. If you're too successful, however, the contact may not feel like she has much to contribute. By explicitly sharing how you will benefit from the potential advisor's expertise, however, you highlight other people's value to you and significantly increase the likelihood they will support you.

3. **Put a time boundary on the advising relationship.** To set and manage expectations for everyone (both you and the advisor), ask if they would be willing to advise you over the next several months or a year. This time limit makes it less onerous for someone to become an advisor, and it preserves your flexibility to exit an advising relationship that turns out not to be useful. You will be able to let relationships "expire" or return for an additional commitment.

When individuals do agree to be advisors, be direct and honest about the challenges you are facing. For example, share that you are not sure what to do about a troublesome employee or about the company's strategy or about an ongoing negotiation. If the relationship goes well, then you might consider inviting the advisor onto your board.

Tip #38: Recruit a Board Based on the Three Ws (Work, Wealth and Wisdom)

A board of directors is often a legal requirement for formal organizations, whether for-profit or nonprofit. They can do much good or much harm (or nothing at all). While some board members will have great wisdom, experience, and connections to share, others will have their own agendas, which might conflict with your vision and with the true goals of your startup. Because board members will have voting power and will exercise a measure of control over your startup, it is crucial to recruit board members very carefully. Keep in mind these considerations:

1. **You need to know what you want your board to do, and you need to identify each board member's specific role.** If you think someone has the potential to become a helpful, supportive, and valuable board member, invite that person onto an advisory council first. Working with the person initially as an advisor will give you a sense of whether the potential you saw can be realized. It will also help you determine whether the person has the time to invest as a member of the board, as well as whether she will work well with or complement the contributions of other existing board members. (*See Tip #26 about seeking complementary skill sets among your co-founders.*)

2. **Grant board membership based on three criteria: Work, Wealth, and Wisdom.** These are the three key types of contribution that board members can make. Potential board members should demonstrate *at least two of the three Ws.*

    -   *Work.* These board members put in time and energy that materially contribute to the startup. They may help draft legal, financial, or strategic documents; they may help develop and refine prototypes; or they may help expand your network significantly. Board members are often valuable because they bring skills (such as legal or financial or technical skills) before you have the ability to hire staff.

    -   *Wealth.* These board members are willing and able to inject financial value into the startup. They not only may supply some of the seed funding, but they also can connect you to other funding sources. If you are counting on board members to help you raise funds, you must make sure that they themselves have made an investment or donation to the startup. If they don't invest themselves, they will not be effective fundraisers.

- *Wisdom.* These board members provide advice and expertise related to the startup's strategy, operations, or organizational development. They may also have relevant industry experience and knowledge. The more reputable and well-established these individuals are in your field of operations, the better.

3. **You should also assess their level of commitment.** If someone provides valuable work, wealth, or wisdom on just one occasion, that may be nice, but it does not demonstrate sufficient commitment to warrant board membership. Occasionally, there will be a prominent individual whose name alone adds luster to your enterprise and who allows you to leverage her credibility when you approach outsiders. You might also have a board member who is happy to write a big check, but is otherwise uninvolved with the organization. There are merits to having such individuals associated with your startup. In general, however, you want board members who will also roll up their sleeves.

Once the board members are recruited, don't forget about them. Involve them in specific tasks, and show them that they are an important part of your organization. With co-founders, advisors, board members, possibly early investors, and others now involved in your startup, you'll need to effectively manage all of these people. The next chapter is devoted to highlighting specific techniques to lead your growing and diverse team.

PART SIX

HOW TO LEAD YOUR STARTUP AND MANAGE YOUR TEAM

HOW TO LEAD YOUR STARTUP AND MANAGE YOUR TEAM

I haven't managed people or been responsible for an entire organization before. How do I manage my team so we all work well together? How can I give critical feedback in a way that doesn't sap morale? How can I continue to motivate my team so they do the best they can?

The skills to manage a team are different from those required to build one. Once I built a robust group of advisors, board members, and team members to get the AWLU idea moving, I faced new challenges. I had to manage everyone in a coordinated effort, retain some control over organizational direction, and make sure that work got done, especially when not everyone was fully paid. Another specific challenge was balancing the emotional tasks of inspiring faith in the AWLU vision while also critiquing the work of others, holding them accountable, and motivating higher levels of productivity. This was incredibly difficult. You will need to overcome similar challenges. This chapter provides communication and team management strategies that will help you maximize the commitments and contributions of the team you have painstakingly built.

$\infty\!\!\!\ll\!\!\!\infty$

Tip #39: Facilitate
(It's Your Bread and Butter)

Everyone knows that the job of the founder is to delegate, but you also need to facilitate. If you have done a good job recruiting, you will have assembled a team of individuals who are energetic and talented, many of whom may have more knowledge or expertise in a particular domain than you do. Facilitating means both using your convening power to bring together talented individuals together and providing the structure and space for them to do their best work. The following principles enable you to be an effective facilitator, whether in face-to-face or virtual meetings:

1. **Do not be the know-it-all**. You are not be an expert in everything and you shouldn't claim to be the smartest one in the room. In fact, you should strike a tone that says, *"You are all experts in your own areas, and that's why we are all here. Let's imagine what we can do together."* You just need to be familiar enough with the matter at hand to keep the meeting on track, to focus others on the key issues, to mediate tensions, and to identify (and track) follow-up steps.

2. **Circulate a tentative meeting agenda and invite others to add to it.** The agenda should indicate the purpose or goal of each meeting and the expectations of who will speak and for how long. Once the agenda is set, keep to the schedule as reasonably possible. For example, you might say, *"We're going to present the material, then we'll have 10 minutes to discuss, and then we will move on."* You can enforce speaking times, for example, by saying, *"I am sorry, Mike, but your time is nearly up. Please summarize your remarks in another minute."* If you need to, agree to modify the agenda or continue the discussion offline or another time.

3. **Set norms and expectations.** Good facilitators establish and maintain a positive working culture. While it may seem hokey, having a work culture discussion before there is a conflict will mitigate tensions when they inevitably arise (*see Tip #68 on expecting conflict*). Team members should generate the norms themselves and express whatever they would like to see from the

group at the beginning of the work relationship. Norms can be as basic as *"show up on time"* or *"respond to emails within 24 hours"* or *"show respect for each other's ideas and opinions."* Also, agree on a regular interval to revisit shared norms and expectations. The norms are less important than the space you create for such conversations in the future about how the group will work together. If that conversation is part of your regular routine, you will be able to address potential misunderstandings before they drive destructive wedges between people. Co-founders should engage in similar discussions before penning their founders' operating agreement (*see also Tip #26 on how to recruit co-founders*).

4. **Handle thorny issues by focusing on facts or tabling the discussion for later.** Inevitably, some issues will cause contentious debate, with members talking at cross-purposes. When this happens, prompt people to move from opinions and value statements to discussions about facts and options. Maintain a focus on guiding principles, such as what is in the best interest of the startup. Do not let conversations "go negative" as this rarely resolves issues. If a tough conversation does not reach a resolution, table it (diplomatically) and continue it later.

5. **Before closing out the meeting, ask participants what help they need from others.** Close a discussion by highlighting areas of agreement and restating agreed upon decisions. Make sure, however, to ask whether the responsible party needs help from others on the team. Asking this provides additional insurance that members will follow through on their commitments. You will then need to follow up on these matters. (*See Tip #42 about offering support to preempt or address underperformance.*)

Good advance work takes almost as much time as the meeting itself. Prepare meeting logistics, agendas, and next steps carefully. (*See also Tip #69 on how to steer meetings and decisions.*) These may seem like small details, but without planning, it will be hard to coordinate an effective working group that can produce the next, best thing. But as much as you want to coordinate, you should also balance your desire to control.

Tip #40: Foster Collaboration and Creativity

Founders often have intense personalities and a powerful sense of vision and direction. You must be careful not to alienate your team by seeming overly controlling. If you want your partners, employees, and volunteers to remain committed and enthusiastic, you must give them a sense of autonomy and some voice in the organization. Show them that their input is valued, even if their suggestions are not always incorporated into the final decision. Here are some ways you can do so:

1. **Ask "What do you think?"** Asking this at the end of an email or a conversation ensures that others feel included in the direction of the startup. It also allows you to test their receptivity to your proposal. This is especially important when you need buy-in from indispensable or senior members of your team. Of course, you won't always agree with all of their feedback, but you can find a way to take what you do agree with and embed it in the final decision. Don't forget to speak publicly about how their feedback influenced the final decision. Your startup goals will come to fruition if your team has a common vision and values – and all the more so when their input is both invited and acknowledged.

2. **Say "Great idea!"** When someone proposes an idea, identify an aspect of the idea that you agree with – even if it is not the whole thing – and say "great idea"; then describe what you like about it and suggest ways that you might be able to incorporate that idea into your strategy. Even if you completely disagree with someone's idea, say "interesting idea" with as much sincerity and enthusiasm as you can muster. Whichever phrase you use, always ask for clarification and never dismiss an idea out of hand. These phrases signal your respect and support, and having more information enables you to adjust your approach and to evaluate the other person's approach responsibly.

    For example, Olga Kotsur is the founder of Mercaux, a startup that has developed a technology to improve the effectiveness of in-store retail sales forces. Olga initially thought she needed to be diligent, study potential partner companies in detail, and seek a warm introduction before reaching out. When a junior person on her team suggested that they simply make a short simple pitch and cold call potential partners, Olga was skeptical, but said "interesting idea" and allowed the junior person to try her approach. As Olga said, *"I didn't think it would work, but it turned out to be a super effective strategy. I ended up learning that I didn't have to spend a lot of time on due diligence. And it was good for the self-development of the employee and good for the company that she took initiative. It turned out potential partners could immediately see the value in partnering and those who didn't reply were lower priority contacts."* No one wants to feel like a mere cog who mechanically accepts directives and churns out work product.

3. **Recognize and reward.** Being an entrepreneur often requires doing as much as possible with very little. Frankly, this means exploiting what is available, including whatever talent is at your disposal. For example, you may ask team members to stay late or to accept a lower salary than they really deserve. Especially in a social enterprise, team members tend to be idealistic, selfless and willing to work long hours for the good of the cause, even with minimal compensation. If you take advantage of people's goodwill for too long, however, the whole arrangement will eventually collapse under the weight of resentment and disillusionment. Strive to offer appropriate rewards and recognition as soon as you can, and before people have to voice their dissatisfaction. Recognizing and rewarding helps you retain your startup team members and cements their commitment.

4. **Care before work.** Theodore Roosevelt famously said, "People don't care how much you know until they know how much you care." Take time to show interest in people before getting to the work. It's easy to become so focused on your startup goals or on the immediate tasks at hand that you forget that your team members are people with lives and concerns outside of work. These are a few ways to show you care:

    •   Instead of jumping onto calls or into meetings and talking immediately about work, first ask how everyone is doing, if everyone had a good weekend, or if they managed to celebrate a holiday.

- If possible, make reference to something that someone has said in a previous meeting or conversation, thus showing that it has been on your mind.

- Take the time to announce and celebrate any major good news in someone's life.

- Keep in mind (and reference) someone's career or graduate school goals or outside interests, and share relevant information or contacts.

This approach might sound inefficient, wasteful, and unproductive. It might feel frustrating because you will have to slow down, shift gears, and focus for a few minutes on seemingly mundane matters, even though you are eager to delve into pressing matters. But there is value in engaging on a personal level, since personal connection is precisely what motivates people to stay with your startup and work hard.

Being collaborative can sometimes feel frustrating. At first you will be accustomed to exercising initiative unilaterally, working alone or with a small and scrappy team of co-founders. But bear in mind that "you can go fast alone or far together." Through the sometimes cumbersome process of collaboration, your startup will achieve greater success over time than if you acted on your own, and even if things don't always go flawlessly the first time.

MAGIC WORDS:

Need to be a better collaborator? Tack on these four magic words "What do you think?" at the end of a sentence or an email and watch... Instantly, people will view you as more collaborative. And you will have gained some additional insight as well. Sprinkle these four words liberally!

Tip #41: Let Your Team Make Early Mistakes

As the founder, you will want to maximize every opportunity and you will have very high standards for yourself and for others on your team. Others, however, may not always accomplish tasks according to your standards or expectations.

1. **Rather than pointing out every flaw or criticizing every minor failure, be prepared to accept some level of imperfection.** For example, you might be trying raise funds from investors, and one of your co-founders might want to do the pitch. Even though she might not be as effective at pitching as you are, you should allow her to do it and not point out every minor way the pitch could have gone better.

    Lisa Walker was the founder of LearningInSync. Lisa wanted to create a virtual library of bilingual books, and she had delegated the responsibility of selecting the books to a co-founder. However, Lisa was displeased with his choices and criticized his decisions. As Lisa says, *"Looking back, I understand how my reaction discouraged my co-founder from making further suggestions. I should have let him run with his own selections so he could gain experience and expertise on his own. I ended up selecting the content myself, even though I didn't have the time to make careful selections."*

2. **By accepting some suboptimal performance, you build your startup team's experience, skills, and confidence in whatever task is at hand.** You can highlight what has been done well without necessarily calling out every mistake, so that people feel psychologically safe to take initiative. This will serve you in the long run, since you can't be everywhere at once and will need your teammates to take on the responsibilities that you alone cannot shoulder.

Still, don't let all shortcomings slip by. You need to make sure your team members are getting the job done, and that requires tact.

Tip #42: Address Underperformance Diplomatically

New, young founders often rely on the goodwill of others to support their startup efforts. Friends and family may contribute time and effort without direct compensation, and even employees may work for less than competitive salaries or forgo options to work elsewhere. In order to nourish their commitment and motivation, you must show consistent appreciation, gratitude, and tact, especially when addressing a potential problem.

1. **Point out problems by asking questions.** Frame trouble spots as matters to be investigated rather than as problems to be fixed. When you encounter a trouble spot in someone's work, ask if the person also notices a potential problem.

    For example, Florence Dennis, the founder of an African snack company, noticed that the corn used in her snack was inconsistent in softness and chewiness. But Florence wanted her snack to be produced with predictable quality. She needed to raise this "corn issue" carefully with her mother and siblings who were helping with her company. As Florence says, *"I didn't want to seem ungrateful for their involvement, so my strategy was to ask for their opinion on the matter: Did they think the product was consistent in texture? Should the consistency be improved, and if so, how could it be done?"*.

    By showing respect for their opinions, she was able to spark their motivation to identify and address the problem. They ended up solving the problem by having a supplier – an aunt – go to the village to secure specific corn varieties rather than just accepting any kind of corn. This approach solved the consistency problem, and Florence preserved her good relationship with her family members.

    By investigating problems, individuals save face and don't have to be "called out" on their mistakes. You also can save face yourself in case you incorrectly perceived a problem that wasn't one.

2. **Remind team members of their responsibility and of why fulfilling it is good for them.** When someone simply doesn't follow through on a responsibility, remind the person of

her earlier commitments and describe how fulfilling those commitments will be good for her as well as for the enterprise. Explicitly say, *"It will be good for you!"*

For example: *"Hey James, you said you were going to work on that logo. Do you know when you will be able to finish it? We are looking forward to using it on the website and it will be good for you to add it to your portfolio of work."* Good leaders recognize that people have their own interests and appeal to them to meet both the needs of their organization and of their team members. (*See also Tip #28 discussing how money isn't everything, Tip #36 on building stakeholder interest, and Tip #64 on focusing on what's in it for others.*)

3. **Offer support when (or even before) you sense trouble looming.** When you delegate a task that may be somewhat challenging, or whenever you sense that trouble is looming, offer team members assistance by asking, *"How can I support you?"* or saying, *"Please tell me how I can support you."* This question invites people to consider and describe what specific conditions would help them to improve their performance or their productivity.

    The word "support" is a code word for "help." When offered help, people may feel relieved, less alone, and more motivated to succeed, since they know they can come to you. They also will have less of an excuse for any poor performance later, since you will have encouraged them to seek out and take advantage of support.

4. **Ask if this is someone's "best work."** In some cases, you might not be in a reasonable position to help or, despite many rounds of feedback, you might still be dissatisfied with the results so far. As options seem to narrow, pose the following question, politely but directly: *"Is this the best that you can do?"* This question is essentially a challenge to the person to think out of the box and to pursue the most creative or sophisticated solutions she can think of on her own. Asking for someone's "best" is an appeal to personal pride and professionalism, and it increases the likelihood of generating the person's best work.

5. **Offer constructive guidance rather than give feedback.** When feedback cannot be communicated effectively in the form of

questions, you will have to be more direct. Ask if the person would like some "guidance" rather than asking if she would like "feedback." The word "guidance" is more inviting and makes people feel less defensive than the word "feedback" which has a more negative connotation.

When offering "guidance", emphasize people's current value and then indicate that they would become even more valuable if they incorporated certain suggestions.

For example, Jerrit Tan is the CEO of Canopy Apps, a company that provides quick translations of medical terms and instructions for doctors and patients. One of Jerrit's employees was highly skilled technically, but he would sometimes explode in anger when he expressed his views, and he would criticize his colleagues publicly, prompting resentment. Clearly, Jerrit needed to have a conversation with this person about showing more consideration for his colleagues. However, Jerrit valued this person's technical skill greatly, and he worried that any negative feedback would hurt their relationship. Jerrit found that suggesting what the person could do to become more valuable was more effective than telling the person what not to do.

Sure, one might be tempted to say something direct like, "*Hey Mike, you're incredibly skilled at programming, but you have to stop criticizing people in public and yelling. It is hurting morale and your relationships with others.*"

A better approach, however, might be: "*Hey Mike, the technical skills you bring to our company are truly valuable, AND you would be even more valuable to us if you could provide feedback so that people are more receptive to it. When you have suggestions for others, I want to encourage you to offer these suggestions calmly and in private to begin with. I think that will make the team more cohesive and the company even more successful.*"

Constructive guidance both highlights someone's value and suggests additional positive behaviors that the person can adopt to increase her value to the team.

Whenever you work with a group, you will notice potential trouble spots in other people's work, or someone who is not fulfilling her responsibilities. But even if no one is underperforming, you'll need to notice when to equip others to assume greater levels of responsibility beyond their initial skill or comfort level.

Tip #43: Groom and Be Groomed

It is unlikely that you will start out with a team of all-stars from the get-go. More likely, your startup will initially be comprised of a ragtag team of friends or young people with energy, time, and enthusiasm for the project. In order to maximize the available talent on your team, you will need to grow everyone's skills, from the most junior to the most senior members of your startup, yourself included.

1. **Groom yourself by inviting others to advise and coach you and by taking on new experiences.** Unless you are a serial entrepreneur who already has experienced significant success with prior startups, it is likely that you yourself will not be highly experienced in your venture's industry or area. Despite your status as founder, encourage even junior members of the team to provide you with constructive feedback. You will be surrounded by them on a daily basis and will benefit from their observations and feedback.

2. **Groom individuals in your startup who show promise by giving them greater responsibility and supporting them in their new responsibility.** For example, you might ask someone to take on more challenging responsibilities (such as becoming the direct contact to a high profile potential funder). To groom someone to take on the new responsibility, simultaneously (a) provide support (perhaps by being present with them at the first formal meeting or by supplying talking points), and (b) break down the new responsibility into discrete steps (such as guiding the person to first research the investor, then to create a pitch deck, and then finally to schedule the meeting).

    Olga Kotsur of Mercaux had a small team and needed someone who could also take on a sales role. She identified a promising employee who was highly effective at managing client relationships with existing clients. This employee, however, did not have experience in sales and was not comfortable with certain aspects of the sales process, like generating leads and making initial contact. But, Olga said, *"I broke down the sales process into discrete steps: I gave her ideas of how to generate potential sales leads, I gave her template emails to make the initial contact, and I gave her goals of how many people to contact and how many prospects to have conversations with each week. I had her record what happened on each call, and we would review the outcomes of those conversations and discuss what went well and what went wrong. Now she can manage the sales process even though she wasn't able to create that process for herself."*

3.   **Even senior members will need to be groomed.** Although you might have older, more established, and professionally successful members on your team, you should not assume that they do not need to be groomed. For example, the fact that some board members are wealthy or powerful does not mean that they know how to fundraise effectively, especially if they do not have startup experience themselves. Fortunately, the techniques described above will work for more established team members, too.

Plan for the long term: since you can't do everything yourself, you will need your team to take on more and more responsibilities. As long as everyone is learning and growing, your team and your startup will benefit.

Tip #44: Counter Startup Stagnation

During the initial stages of your startup, you will gather a team of individuals with various strengths and capabilities. They might advance your startup in meaningful ways, such as in fundraising or developing a highly innovative prototype. Over time, however, you might notice that your fundraising has leveled off or that you are not able to produce a satisfactory technical product even after trying many different approaches. To overcome any slump or stagnation, and to amplify your team's resources, you'll need to bring in new members who can jolt you out of the slump.

1. **Guard against stagnation by constantly assessing the adequacy of your enterprise's human capital.** To assess human capital, heed the saying that the "proof is in the pudding." If you don't see individuals making significant progress for a sustained period of time (say, eight to twelve months), even after trying many different approaches, you will need to add someone to your team who has more experience, skills, or connections in the area where you are having difficulty. Don't be complacent. The skills and stature of your team should always be growing.

2. **Recruit new team members who bring additional or different value (in terms of status, connections, resources, or skill sets).** Identify who on your team has the highest social status (or skill set or connections) and aim to recruit someone with at least equal talents or assets. Deliberately investigate your highest level contacts, and then set out to cultivate and recruit some fresh connections and talent.

3. **This process can feel threatening to existing team members, as they may fear being displaced, demoted, or sidelined in their areas of responsibility, as you bring in new people.** In such cases, subtly reassure your team that you are not trying to drive anyone out (if that is the case). Point out the recent stagnation and emphasize that the new person brings useful skills, resources, or connections that will build on the team's existing strength and launch the startup to the next level of success. This success will benefit everyone.

Leadership in maintaining and expanding your team will put you in all sorts of potentially awkward and stressful situations. But it is part of your job to keep everyone calm and cognizant of the collective goal to create a business that doesn't flop.

Tip #45: Keep Your Eye on the Ball

New founders are often required to move fast and in multiple directions because there is so much to do. Over time, however, you will need to prioritize activities related to your primary goal of setting up a *sustainable business*, one that earns revenue (even if that revenue comes in the form of donations). If you lose sight of that goal, then your startup will not survive, and you will not be in a position to solve problems, improve lives, or do the good you want to see in the world. Here are some ways to keep focused:

1. **Once you gain traction, protect your time.** New founders must often devote huge amounts of time to networking. They are enthusiastic and they can get an energy high from such activities. However, once you have built your team and made the relevant contacts, you can afford to focus your energy on specific objectives (e.g., recruiting a co-founder or hiring a developer). Stop attending events or taking meetings that aren't within the scope of your new priorities. Focus on the work of building the business, and don't spread yourself too thin.

2. **Make money, not scientific discoveries.** Engineers or technically oriented individuals are often susceptible to tunnel vision. For example, Joseph Walish co-founded Thermeleon, Inc., a company that attempted to develop a rooftop coating that would be white during the summer (to reflect heat) and change to black during the winter (to absorb heat).

    As Joseph says, "*I spent more than eight years during and after graduate school trying to get the technology to work. Even after all that time there was always 'one more idea' that I could pursue to make it work. We were making progress, but eventually it became more like a research project rather than a startup.*" If he had kept his eye on the ball, he would have more quickly seen that he was not reaching the goal of generating revenue and could have pivoted to a more promising startup idea. (*See Tip #15 on not getting so stuck to a first idea.*) If you can't get your technology to work after several iterations, move onto a different idea. Neither your time nor your resources are infinite.

3. **Make sales, not friends.** Similarly, Zac Aghion, the founder of Splitforce, also became distracted from his startup objectives at times. He would engage in a soft sell, talking to potential clients about their problems and brainstorming how they might leverage his software. Many times, he quickly understood that someone was not going to buy the product; but because he was so passionate about helping people solve problems, sales calls would turn into free, hour-long consulting sessions. Move on if prospects say they doesn't have one of five things: the budget, authority, interest, need or timeline for your product – unless someone describes changing circumstances that might enable an investment or sale.

The pressure to create a sustainable business is enormous, especially when you have traction and individuals whose payroll you must make. How do you maintain and convey emotional strength in the face of such pressures?

Tip #46: Exercise Emotional Leadership

Leadership requires a high level of emotional commitment. But when it comes to the daily grind of getting things done, making decisions, and resolving conflicts, leaders often need to temper their emotions and instead project a calm, low-key and even unflappable attitude.

Especially when you or others are feeling upset, frustrated or angry, you will need to rise above the emotional upheavals to restore peace in the realm. And when something unexpected and undesirable happens, your demeanor must suggest that nothing has caught you off guard (even when it has!). Your team will rely on you for reassurance, even when you yourself are worrying about next month's payroll or about snagging a major partnership that will keep the startup afloat.

To serve as the voice of calm, try some of these techniques:

1. **Use a calm and measured tone of voice.** Especially during tense times, speak slowly and calmly. Control the tempo of your words and how high you raise your voice. You should also avoid superlatives (such as "so" and "very"), absolutes (such as "all," "none," or "never") and inflammatory language.

2. **Add levity to relieve the pressure.** When the group is riled up about something, you can interject this phrase with a subdued but humorous tone: *"There's no need for a panic attack."* It's a mildly funny phrase, it can apply to many different situations, and it helps the group to see things in perspective. You will be able to reduce tension and quickly bring the group back together.

3. **Focus on gathering information.** During times of distress, calmly ask others for clarification about what has happened and direct them to explore the possible courses of action. Posing questions allows members to focus their attention on facts and what you know (or what you need to know), rather than on the emotional distress.

4. **Reframe setbacks as positive developments.** Rather than reacting to bad news, simply and matter-of-factly acknowledge the disappointment, but also point out a silver lining. If possible, announce a promising new path or an opportunity to overcome the disappointment. Alternatively, describe why the

disappointment allows the startup to avoid an even less favorable situation down the road.

5. **Keep bad news at bay until it needs to be shared.** In the midst of a crisis, you might choose not to share all the details as they are happening. For example, if you fail to receive a key approval, contract or investment that you were counting on, you might wait until you are certain that these opportunities are lost, until you have identified a silver lining, or until you have an alternative plan of action. There is a fine line to walk, because you need to be the beacon of optimism while also maintaining reasonable transparency. At some point, you have to acknowledge challenges in order to address them effectively as a team.

Now that you know how to maintain emotional calm, you'll also need to incorporate an ethical compass in your leadership.

BE THE THERMOSTAT:

The best founders retain a sense of calm amid both the lows and highs of startup life. Founders must carefully modulate their emotional states based on the emotional levels of others and the circumstances confronting their startups. Don't be a thermometer; be the thermostat and set the temperature in the room accordingly.

Tip #47: Exercise Moral Leadership

As you seek to advance your startup in the high-pressured world of entrepreneurship, there may be times when your ethical compass is challenged. Many young founders don't expect to face ethical dilemmas, have not found themselves in such situations before, and are caught off guard when they find themselves in such a predicament.

If you find yourself in circumstances where the very survival of your startup is at stake, you may be tempted to do things that you would not ordinarily do. To prepare to face these temptations, consider the following ideas:

1. **Be clear in advance about which ethical lines you personally are not willing to cross.** For example, you might decide that you will not accept investments from dubious sources or exaggerate financial performance in order to sell your startup. By marking such lines for yourself in advance, you shield yourself from the temptation to cross them later.

2. **Instill ethical values into your startup from the beginning.** Directly introduce ethical values by talking with your team about what you stand for, what the startup mission is about, and what principles your startup represents. Anticipate some potential dilemmas that you or your startup might find yourself in. Even if these scenarios don't arise, some thought will prepare you better for the scenarios that do.

3. **When you face a particular ethical dilemma, research and reflect.** Identify the values or ethical principles that, in your view, are most relevant to the issue at hand, and consider why you might prioritize one value over another. Consider your personal motivations and evaluate how your self-interest colors your assessment of the situation (if at all).

    Also, assess the impact your actions might have on others and how you would feel if your actions were reported in the newspaper. You might also seek out a trustworthy neutral party and ask for advice. You can even try to search for articles discussing your specific dilemma. Analyze the ways you might be able to reap reasonable benefits for your startup without betraying your core values and without crossing your ethical boundaries.

Finally, if it seems you must pursue unethical measures, that might signal that your startup idea was not meant to survive or not the best one to stake your future on.

It is likely that your ethical boundaries will be challenged in some way over the life of the startup. Encountering these situations may in fact be a sign of your startups' progress, since it means that there are real benefits at stake. An ethical culture within your startup, however, generates loyalty among your team members, inspires long-term support, and makes your efforts worthwhile. Now that you know how to support your team to do its best work in a collaborative and sometimes high stakes setting, the next chapter focuses on how to engage with external partners, customers, and investors.

PART SEVEN

HOW TO MAKE YOUR FIRST SALE OR KEY PARTNERSHIP

HOW TO MAKE YOUR FIRST SALE OR KEY PARTNERSHIP

I'm looking to make my first sale and secure my first key partnership. How do I get in touch with the individuals and organizations that can potentially support, invest in, or partner with us? How do I effectively present a proposal so it'll be positively received by prospective customers or partners? How do I get people to give me a timely response?

Naturally in trying to establish a global women's leadership university, we wanted the support of a woman leader, such as Hillary Clinton. We also dreamed of support from individuals like Michael Bloomberg, but we didn't know how to get close to such high-profile people – they seemed out of reach for us. We also wanted institutional and corporate support, but we didn't know who we should be reaching out to at places like Bloomberg LP (the media company and the foundation) or Goldman Sachs. Even when we had an idea of whom we wanted to reach, we didn't necessarily have their contact information. Don't be deterred, however, if you have your eye on certain individuals or organizations whose support would be valuable, these tips will help. Connect with whoever has the most decision-making power, and know that the contact information you need isn't as unavailable as you think.

$\infty\!\!\times\!\!\infty$

Tip #48: Reach out to the "Big Four" Contacts

Although young founders often look for anyone they can get to or feel most comfortable reaching out to junior people, you should aim high and reach out to the most important contact possible. Your networking efforts should be leading you toward four key categories of contacts in order of importance: Head Honchos, Decision-Makers, Key Influencers, and Internal Champions. (Note that one contact might exemplify two or more of these categories. For example, someone might be a Head Honcho as well as a Decision-Maker. A Key Influencer might also serve as an Internal Champion.) Raising funds and striking mutually beneficial partnerships are both relationship-building processes and a numbers game.

1. **Head Honcho.** The Head Honcho is the most senior person in an organization, such as the CEO or Chairman of the Board. If you can persuade this person to support your startup, the organization or others will have to follow suit. Be aware, however, that this person may delegate decision-making power to a less senior Decision-Maker.

2. **Decision-Makers.** Decision-Makers have the authority to expend organizational resources and to approve and execute organizational commitments. For example, they may have the power to approve an investment in or a partnership with your startup. Find out what the formal (and informal) decision-making process is in an organization by *asking about it explicitly*. Ask people within the organization or who have recently worked there, even if you don't know them personally.

3. **Key Influencers.** Key Influencers are individuals who enjoy widespread respect within an organization, even though they might not have a prominent job title or formal decision-making powers relevant to your startup. Perhaps they have been with the organization for a long time or are simply well liked. Whatever the reason, they are regularly consulted for their advice and opinions; thus they can influence Head Honchos and Decision-Makers behind the scenes.

To identify the Key Influencers in any organization (or industry), ask someone who has recently worked for that organization about the most respected or influential individuals there. An online search might reveal which members of the organization are giving interviews, serving as keynote speakers, being referenced or quoted in articles, winning awards, or being showcased on the company website. You can also search online for lists of the most influential individuals in the relevant industry.

4. **Internal Champions.** Internal Champions are people within the organization who are excited about your startup and who are willing to advocate on your behalf with colleagues and superiors, especially with Head Honchos and Decision-Makers. For example, in an investing group or firm, there may be a handful of partners, each of whom will need to agree to invest in your startup. Even if you get one partner excited about your startup, she will need to be armed with information so that she can advocate on your behalf with the rest of the partnership.

    Because they are insiders, Internal Champions know how to test receptivity to an idea or a proposal, and while Internal Champions may not have ultimate or sole decision-making authority, they can provide you with valuable information to which you would not otherwise have access. Internal Champions are not found – they are made: Cultivate relationships with them and get them excited about your startup so that they will want to extend themselves on your behalf. If at all possible, turn a Key Influencer into one of your Internal Champions.

5. **A word about Gatekeepers.** Similar to Decision-Makers are gatekeepers, people who do not have ultimate decision-making authority, but who impact the decision-making process. For example, Chibueze Ihenacho, the founder of ARMR Systems, a medical device company, was trying to raise funds from a notable angel investing group, but he knew his startup would be under the review of the life sciences director. This director was not the ultimate decision-maker as he was not on the board, but he was a gatekeeper. If you can bypass the gatekeeper by winning over someone with more decision-making authority than the gatekeeper, all the better. But be careful not to alienate the gatekeeper in the process.

* Once you have identified your key contacts:

  • **Seek out, if possible, a "warm introduction"** where you ask someone the contact knows and respects to introduce you. Friends working at a company can make an introduction for you, but be aware that this request might put them in the awkward position of "sticking out their necks" for you at a time when they are focused on demonstrating their own value to the company. "Corporate-types" – especially junior individuals working in large organizational structures – tend to be risk averse and to respect hierarchy, and may not be well positioned to persuade a senior person of the value of a new idea or a new product.

  • **Even if you don't have a warm introduction, you should in most cases reach out directly to the most senior person you can connect with.** A senior executive, who has an eye on the horizon and understands the full scope of the company, is best positioned to recognize the value of a new product or new innovation related to her business. She can make quick decisions herself or connect you to the right person (who will be more likely to favorably consider your idea).

The more ways you have to link up with a potential supporter the better, especially when you are trying to reach the most exclusive and elusive folks. The next tip provides some insights about connecting to the people you need.

THE BIG FOUR:

Don´t be afraid to reach out to the most senior people in an organization. Always aim to connect with the Big Four:

- **Head Honcho**: runs the organization and is either CEO or Chairman of the Board!
- **Decision-Makers**: has authority over the decision-making process.
- **Key Influencers**: doesn´t have official authority over the decision-making process but they can influence it.
- **Internal Champion**: can advocate for your startup to senior members in the organization.

Tip #49: Identify Six Points of Contact

Sometimes you won't be able to reach out directly to the key contact whose support you want or need, because that person will be too senior or too elusive. Don't give up. In such cases, identify and reach out to six individuals within the desired contact's social circle, and ensure that those six individuals know about and become enthusiastic about your startup.

1. **Be a detective. Figure out who is in your key contact's social circle.** Google the organizations she is a part of and news articles about her. Find out what panels she has spoken on, and what events she supports or attends. Six points of contact might include a board member in an organization with which the key contact is involved, an employee at the key contact's company, a parent whose child attends the same school as the key contact's child, a member of the congregation at the key contact's synagogue or church, or even a relative, friend, or spouse of the key contact. Don't worry about the stature of your six points of contact; you're simply trying to find six individuals who naturally circulate in the key contact's social or professional networks.

2. **Once you make a connection with these six points of contact, get them excited about your startup.** If they aren't excited about your startup, they aren't the right contacts for you – you're not looking to change people's minds, but to inform and connect. Most likely, they will cross paths with your intended key contact, and they may be willing to recommend you or even introduce you to the key contact, or at the very least mention your startup to her. Hearing about your idea from a familiar and trustworthy source increases the chance that your key contact will be receptive to your startup when you do manage to connect with her.

Perhaps this all seems circular, needing contacts to get contacts. How might you break the ice in the first place and get a response? For example, how might you reach people you want to know via email?

Tip #50: Use Email Permutations

Many new founders get stumped when they come across the profile of an interesting person online but can't find an email address on the website. The solution is simple: if you can't obtain an introduction through your existing network or find an email address online, try various email permutations, such as jane.doe@company.com, jdoe@company.com, president@company.com, or doe.jane@company.com.

For example, Michael Schmidt, the founder of Vaska Technologies, wanted to reach out to CEOs of companies that manufactured coffee machines, hoping to spark an interest in his technology that would automate the replenishment of coffee pods. However, a CEO's email address was not always listed on a company's website. Although Michael had friends working at one of these coffee machine manufacturing companies, he was not comfortable asking them to share the CEO's email address. While he could sometimes find a CEO with whom he had an alumni connection, he couldn't necessarily find the CEO's email address in the alumni database. Undeterred, Michael decided to figure out an email address with intelligent guesswork. He would peruse a company's website and notice that the **email format** for that company might be firstname.lastname@company.com or some other permutation. He would then try half a dozen permutations. While some of his emails would bounce back, eventually one of his emails would go through.

In addition, individuals are often part of multiple organizations – they may sit on one board and also serve in different capacities for two or more other organizations. If you can't obtain the contact information from one organization or can't get through to the individual through email permutations based on that organization, check on LinkedIn to see **what other organizations the person is currently affiliated with**. Use email permutations based on that other organization's email format to double your attempts to connect with the individual. You can also send messages directly to the person through LinkedIn.

Finally, it is important that you **download Streak** or another email tracking program so you can monitor whether an email has been read. Of course, once you connect with individuals, you'll need to convince them that you have something that they want.

Tip #51: Get the Sale Before Producing

In sales, it used to be that you would produce your product and then peddle your wares to prospective clients. Instead of adhering to this old-fashioned method, consider confirming first with prospective clients that they would be interested in the product if it were available. Kickstarter, in fact, is built entirely on this strategy and has allowed a host of entrepreneurs to **validate the market interest** in their products and to collect funding from future customers in advance.

This doesn't mean you should stall decisions to produce an MVP (minimum viable product) or an early "beta" version so you can show individuals what you hope to sell. But many founders hole-up in their laboratories and delay the process of getting feedback. Don't stay stuck in your own idea! Get out there and test market interest:

1. **Sell your product before you produce your product.** For example, Jerrit Tan had started a tee-shirt company with two friends in college. They were into fashion and felt they could create innovative and popular tee-shirt designs. Initially, they planned to design the tees, get them printed, send samples to stores, and sell their first season. They soon realized that carrying inventory was expensive. Later, they learned to create an online catalogue where people could view the tee-shirt designs and put in orders. By doing so, they avoided costs associated with making and distributing samples, producing and keeping inventory, and creating and printing catalogues. You should similarly gauge interest before producing your product.

2. **Make hypothetical sales to gauge consumer interest in your product.** For example, Ben Jabbawy is the founder of Privy.com. When Ben first launched his startup, he talked with 30 business owners in his neighborhood and received positive feedback on the usefulness of his technology that tracked how social media campaigns led to in-store revenue. He went home and drew mockups for how the technology might work. He then walked back to the business owners, recounted the conversation from the prior week, showed them the hand drawings, and asked whether they would be willing to pilot his technology if he built it. Not surprisingly, they were. In just two months, Ben not only developed the first version of the product and obtained early

feedback, but also found his first paying customers. By making hypothetical sales, you can spark potential customers' interest in your product. Their feedback will also give you insight into their purchasing rationale, which you can use to refine the actual sales pitch when your product is ready.

It's a myth that 'If you build it, people will come.' As much as possible, find out if people will come even if you haven't built it yet. Constantly, and as early as possible, seek out ways to validate market interest in your product or service.

Tip #52: Seek Validation

New founders often think their job is to convince someone that their startup idea is valuable. But they forget about the equally important task of confirming that it is. Don't make a substantial ask (for an investment, collaboration, sale, or partnership) without getting **explicit confirmation** that whatever you are proposing will be of value to the other party.

Before you seek such validation, investigate your prospects' mission, objectives, and strategic initiatives and see how your product or service facilitates them. Once you understand why a prospect would be interested in buying your product, or investing or partnering in your startup, validate your understanding! If your assessment is accurate, you can be pretty sure your pitch will be well received.

1. **Ask whether your product or service furthers your prospect's needs, priorities, or strategic objectives.** Michael Schmidt, the founder of Vaska Technologies, connected to the vice-chairman in charge of strategic initiatives for a company that sold office products, knowing that the company, like many retailers, was worried about competition from Amazon. As Michael says, "*I briefly described my understanding of the company's initiatives to compete with Amazon, and how my technology eliminated the need for consumers to go to Amazon or to any other website to re-order consumables. I then asked whether this technology might support the company's initiative to compete effectively with Amazon. I was able to validate that the company thought automating consumables was beneficial, which paved the way for a conversation about a future partnership.*"

   Be like Michael – do your homework. After describing your understanding of the prospect's priorities and objectives, you can present your product or service to potential customers and ask directly, "*Do you think this would be valuable to your company?*" or "*Is this idea resonating with you?*" (You can even soften this question by saying "*I'm not sure my product is right for you, but...*" This statement is disarming and a nice way to seek validation.) If they say no, ask for their advice about what modifications you could make. This gives you the opportunity to go back to them with those modifications in place. If they say yes, you are then poised for a conversation about a potential sale or investment.

2. **Seek validation by asking for a critique of your startup idea.**
    When you ask for critique, you learn what potential partners
    or investors really think about your work, and can apply their
    suggestions and address their concerns. Chibueze Ihenacho, the
    founder of ARMR Systems, will often say *"You are an experienced
    investor, you've seen lots of deals, what would other investors chew
    me on?"* If they point out a bunch of weaknesses, you'll know
    the areas where you need to get additional data, establish proof
    of concept or beef up your presentation. If they don't have many
    criticisms, you know that they think investing in your startup is a
    sound idea, at least in theory, and you can proceed to a real ask.

3. **Post your idea on a crowdfunding site.** For example, you can
    post on Kickstarter.com, Indiegogo.com, or Microventures.com.
    Not only can you show the product that you're offering to others,
    but you also will get feedback on market interest.

4. **Don't be discouraged if you don't get the validation you were
    hoping for.** You will probably be bad at your business before you
    get good at your business. By seeking validation and hearing how
    your product is falling short, you'll be able to adjust and improve
    your product.

    As you'll recall, Lindsey Hyde started Strong Girls,
    Strong Women and had to create a curriculum for the girls her
    organization was mentoring. As Lindsey says, *"It took a lot of time
    and testing and delivering a curriculum that was embarrassing.
    And that's ok because you have to start somewhere. When we
    created our first curriculum, it was terrible. It had no educational
    value and it wasn't based in research, but it was a good stab for a
    bunch of 19-year-olds, and it was a good starting point. It allowed
    us to test our curriculum and refine it until we had something
    that we were proud of. We weren't best in class until we built our
    business over time."* In new domains, your first attempts will
    likely be disappointing, but if you pay attention to feedback you
    can make steady modifications until you produce something that
    prospective consumers or clients will validate (and will use).

Efforts to validate and refine your product will take you a long way.
Along with getting validation, you will want to research how to address
your particular audience. The next tip will help you develop that skill.

YOUR STARTUP IS A *HYPOTHESIS*:

Remember, your startup is merely a hypothesis. You won't know whether your startup produces products or services that people want until it successfully generates revenue that can sustain the business.

You should have the same humility as Socrates – the only thing you know is that you know nothing. The work of the startup is to collect evidence of the startup idea's growing validity.

Tip #53: Present the Right Interlocutor

The person who presents an idea always influences how well the idea is received. People respond especially positively to those whom they know and trust, who are similar to them, and whom they have met before. Therefore, before every meeting, **consider which of your team members would make the most effective pitch to that particular audience.** Chinese companies use this technique all the time. They know that many Chinese consumers are more receptive to Western-made products. As a result, they hire and showcase Western models in sales and marketing materials to entice Chinese consumers.

Ken Fan is the co-founder of Ad Gene, a company that operates a library of gene samples that researchers can use. In business development meetings, he aims to convince scientists and research centers to share their DNA samples with his company. He understands well how gene samples are collected, stored, tracked, and distributed through the company's DNA storage system. But as he says, "*When I have a meeting trying to convince a scientist to store her gene samples in Ad Gene's library, I will often include a PhD scientist from my staff. I'm fully aware that I may not be perceived as a peer by scientific clients, since I don't hold a doctorate.*"

While this can be uncomfortable at times, consider whether a man, a woman, an older person, a tech-savvy person, a government official or some other kind of specialist would best represent your startup at any particular meeting. (*See also Tip #64 about identifying "what's in it for them" so you frame your conversation to speak to the audience's interests.*) Both *who* you send in and *how* (or when) you send someone in are important to keep in mind, including as it pertains to yourself.

Tip #54: Leverage Yourself as a Big Gun

Young founders often rattle off their accomplishments and credentials in the effort to establish themselves. Even in the early days of your startup, preserve some gravitas for yourself by holding back a little about yourself.

1. **Use your status as the founder or CEO as an angle in sales meetings or other pitches.** For example, a potential client might be meeting with a member of your team, a sales representative. At some point in the conversation, your sales representative might say: *"I'd love to bring my CEO into the conversation to help you think through the vision and to answer additional questions."* People like to feel that they are special. Bringing in the Big Guns, such as the CEO, the founder, or a high-level board member, makes people feel that you are treating them with special consideration.

2. **Reference your unexpected credentials and achievements at chosen moments.** Olga Kotsur, the founder of Mercaux, found that when she met with investors, they were unimpressed by her consulting and finance background. But in the middle of the conversation, she would impress them by casually sharing her technology, physics, and math background. Similarly, when she was talking to the engineers working at a potential client retailer, they were impressed by her understanding of the technology, but were even more impressed when they learned that she developed the idea as a student at Harvard Business School. In both instances, her unexpected background surprised people and gained her additional interest and respect.

Regardless of how you or others present themselves to prospective clients or partners, you'll never know the most effective way to engage with others until you try it.

Tip #55: Experiment in Batches

The early days of a startup involve trial and error. For example, you may have to craft dozens of emails before you come up with a version that generates a positive response (or any response at all). As you experiment with various approaches, try different strategies *systematically* until you find the best method to achieve your goal. (*See also Tip #16 on moving from a pitch to a process.*) Here are some methods for experimenting effectively:

1. **Experiment in batches with the least important contacts first.** If you have hundreds of contacts, experiment first with a small batch of the less prominent ones. Once you figure out what works in reaching out effectively for that batch, replicate the process you've discovered for the next batch of contacts. Working in batches allows you to make mistakes that are only visible to a subset of your potential contacts.

   Jerritt Tan, the CEO of Canopy Apps, wanted to forge partnerships with hospitals so that doctors would be more likely to download the app. Jerritt developed a batch process for generating partnerships. This process involved: generating a list of 50 hospital contacts at a time; sending each one an individually crafted email directed to the Chief Medical Officer (this turned out to be the most effective person to reach out to within the hospital structure); following up two days later; following up again with a cold call if there was still no response; and then finally walking away if nothing had worked.

   Once they figured out what worked within that pool of 50, they refined those emails for the next batch of 50. They proceeded this way until they reached out to 5,500 hospitals in total. Once you find the process that generates the desired outcome, you need to repeat the process systematically to generate partnerships or sales or whatever else you are striving to accomplish (*see Tip #16 on moving from a pitch to a process*).

2. **Use Streak to compose, send out, and monitor emails.** Streak is a customer relationship management platform for Gmail that you can download for free as a Chrome extension. Since you'll be making very similar requests from a great number of people until someone says "yes," you'll be sending a lot of very similar emails,

albeit with some customization. Streak's snippet function allows you to cut and paste the same request very easily, so that when you're knocking on a thousand doors, you're not wearing out a thousand pairs of shoes. Streak also enables you to set reminders for follow-up conversations and to monitor when people open the emails you send to them. It's a great tool for entrepreneurs.

Testing small and using tools like Streak will efficiently perfect your marketing. Getting the word out is great, and you want to make sure your tools and techniques make good use of your time and effort.

Tip #56: Pound the Pavement Effectively

Running a startup requires physical work. It often requires "pounding the pavement," which means making in-person pitches to customers and investors on their turf. If you're not on a plane, bus, car, train, subway, elevator or sidewalk, you may not be doing what needs to be done to advance your start-up. Pounding the pavement requires a significant investment of time, money, and energy.

To maximize your time out of the office, line up meetings in a given city as efficiently as possible. Send out 500 cold emails in order to line up 15 meetings in a particular city during a one-week period by following these steps (and adjusting as appropriate for you):

- *Pick a location and a one-week time period.*
- *Build your contact list.* Use Linkedin or online searches or industry lists to find the companies and contacts that you would like to meet with. Build a spreadsheet of these 500 contacts. (Use a freelancer or assistant if necessary.)
- *Prepare a short outreach email.* This email should contain no more than three to five sentences that (i) offer a greeting and a relevant connection, (ii) indicate that you will be in town for a week during the coming month or two, and (iii) ask whether the recipient would be interested in meeting sometime during that week. You can also include some social proof in your signature block (such as a link to a recent article that has mentioned your startup). (*See Tip #18 about crafting emails that generate a response.*)
- *Delegate the task of sending out the email.* Have your assistant send out a personalized version of the email to each contact, using the contact's name. (*See Tip #54 about leveraging yourself as a big gun. Here you are preserving your status by not sending out the request yourself.*)
- *Schedule the meetings.* If you email 500 contacts and assume a 3% yield rate, you should receive approximately 15 positive responses. Your assistant can then schedule three meetings each day for the week. With 15 scheduled meetings, you can travel to a new city with relative assurance that you'll have a full and meaningful schedule to justify the expense.

Job hunters also often pretend they are going to be in a city and use that as an excuse to land an interview. Similarly, you can email a key contact and say that you will be in their city over a specified period and would love to stop by for a conversation while you're in town – even if you are deliberately flying in just to see that person! The contact will feel less pressure, and thus more inclination, to agree to meet you. Once you have the trip planned, schedule additional meetings in that city, or visits with family and friends, so that your trip will be worthwhile even if your key contact cancels at the last minute.

As you successfully pound the pavement and line up several consecutive meetings or calls, you will not be able nor will you want to follow up on each contact. How can you filter out the least promising leads to avoid chasing a contact who will be a hard sell?

Tip #57: Reach For Low-Hanging Fruit

Because you will cast a wide net as you try to cultivate new relationships, you will need to allocate time and energy carefully, especially when you hope to transform an initial "maybe" into an unqualified "yes." Although you might feel a tenacious determination to turn every contact into an investor or supporter, it is more prudent to focus most of your time on the most promising contacts – the ones who show early signs of real interest and enthusiasm. Don't give up on anyone too soon, but don't waste precious time on a relationship that isn't bearing fruit.

Concentrate on contacts who have a strong, natural alignment with the goals of your startup:

1. **Find people who are already nodding.** Seek out those who have invested in a similar space or cause, already believe in the vision, or are leaning forward, asking questions, and offering suggestions. Not only are these individuals more likely to support your startup, but also they will serve as ambassadors for your startup and open doors for you. In contrast, don't squander time and energy pursuing those who demonstrate skepticism, or with whom you don't connect personally. Ben Rubin, the founder of Change Collective, raised US$1.4 million in a seed round after nine months of persistence and effort. Roger Ying, the founder of Pandai.cn, typically closed deals within two or three meetings.

    Both of these founders agree that once you tell the story of the business, you can tell which people like the story, whether they view you as an expert, and whether there is a sense of trust and comfort between you. Stefanie Botelho, the founder of Fitzroy Toys ("Etsy for toys"), emphasizes that it's important to find people who are willing to back both the person and the space.

2. **Eliminate time wasters.** People who offer advice that is not helpful and people who do not seem interested, but keep asking for proof points and detailed financials are likely to be stringing you along. At the startup stage, your backers should be comfortable taking a risk on you and your new venture. Disconnect and say, *"We've decided not to seek institutional investors at this stage,"* or indicate that you have decided to focus on other priorities. Keep

these people on your list for regular updates, and you can always get in touch again later.

Just because a contact has demonstrated interest in your venture doesn't mean she will always respond to you right away. You will often need to follow up, so learn to craft messages that nudge for feedback in a helpful timeframe without pushing a promising contact away.

Tip #58: Nudge a Timely Response

When pitching to potential partners, investors, or customers, you face a dilemma: You don't want to put people on the spot with a hard deadline, because this risks losing them altogether. At the same time, you require a response within a reasonable amount of time. (*See also Tip #66 on how to follow-up on investor meetings promptly after you have decided to open a fundraising round.*)

Use these non-pushy strategies to elicit an answer or to find out when you can expect one:

1. **Share an internal timeframe:** tell a potential investor that your startup is "*aiming to raise [a certain amount] by [a certain date]*" or "*planning to close the round by [a date]*" (even if the amounts or dates are not written in stone). Ask, "*Would that be enough time for you to make a decision?*" By conveying the timeline for your goal rather than a deadline for their action, you can create a sense of urgency without being too pushy.

2. **Ask them what their "process" is for making a decision.** The word "process" is a euphemism for "When are you going to get back to me?" If people need more time or information, indicate your willingness to try to accommodate their timeframe (so long as it is both reasonable and specific).

3. **When previously warm prospects turn cold, explicitly tell them that you will no longer pursue them.** You might receive some promising signs from a potential investor or partner, only to find that the person stops responding reliably to your subsequent messages. Revive these seemingly lost prospects by writing a friendly, diplomatic email that conveys the following:

   • *Remind the prospect of her earlier enthusiasm for your startup.* Then state that, having reached out multiple times without receiving any response, you assume she must now be too busy or simply no longer interested in a partnership. Add that, in either case, this is not the right time to work together. You can then encourage the person to contact you if she ever has a renewed interest in your startup, and meanwhile, you wish her well. Be sure to keep the email upbeat and polite, without any hint of bitterness or ill will. (*See also Tip #20 on giving easy outs.*)

- A sample email might look like: "*Dear Jane, It was exciting to talk with you last fall, and we thought we had the potential for a great partnership. You seemed really interested in our product. But we've now sent you two emails and called your office twice and haven't heard back. This suggests that you must be very busy at the moment or no longer interested in a partnership. Either way, it seems that this is not a good time for us to work together. If things change on your end, please us know. We wish you the best for the new year.*"

  Such an email might seem like it is simply stating the obvious or beating a dead horse; however, founders report that this strategy elicits a response rate that is 50 percent positive. Perhaps the prospects respond to this email because they feel a little guilty for having ignored you. Perhaps they really have been busy and have been meaning to get back to you, and your email prompts them to do so. Or perhaps, when you say that you will no longer pursue their participation, they suddenly fear losing out on a good opportunity and decide to make their move while there is still time.

  Whatever the reason, such a note motivates elusive prospects to get in on the action before it is too late! And what about those who still do not respond? You will not waste any more time on them, and you will focus on more promising prospects. This strategy is especially appropriate when you have other promising prospects and can afford to lose this particular relationship. It also works when you can no longer wait for a response.

You now know several principles of how to effectively connect with and approach prospective partners – by reaching to the most senior individuals and most interested individuals in a time efficient manner, seeking their explicit validation of the value of your product or service, and getting an answer on whether they will work with you or not. Next, you'll need to learn how to engage another specific and significant group: investors. The next chapter focuses on the unique considerations when asking not for a sale or partnership but a financial investment from others.

PART EIGHT

HOW TO FUNDRAISE FROM INVESTORS (AND DONORS)

HOW TO FUNDRAISE FROM INVESTORS (AND DONORS)

I've never raised money before. How does the fundraising process go? How are startups funded and who is funding them? How do I get people to commit to making an investment? I have never asked other people for money before, and I am uncomfortable with it. What should I do?

When a chance encounter with Peter Grauer, the chair of the Bloomberg board, led to a meeting with the head of Bloomberg Philanthropy in London, we were elated our team was asked to present a funding proposal. But the request caught us off guard – we weren't quite sure what we wanted from Bloomberg Philanthropy! We hadn't yet thought deeply about how to break down our $50 million fundraising goal into bite-sized chunks that would produce appealing short-term results. We also hadn't asked about Bloomberg's comfort level in funding. Finally, we didn't think clearly about Bloomberg's objectives as a foundation and why they would want to fund AWLU in particular. As a result, we didn't hit the right marks, and we squandered an opportunity that was potentially ripe for closure. Like us, you might have only vague notions of why you are fundraising, of how funds might be used, and of the fundraising process itself. In order to effectively raise outside funds, you'll need to decide when and how much to raise; draw up a prospects list; familiarize yourself with some basic finance terminology; and then proceed through an outreach, cultivation, and pitch process. The below tips will equip you to embark on the fundraising process, whether you are a for-profit or nonprofit.

∞

Tip #59: Learn Basic Finance Lingo

Before you reach out to investors, familiarize yourself with basic finance jargon. You do not need to be a finance guru. When you need to learn more about financing, check out Venturehacks.com, Bothsidesofthetable.com, Clerky.com, or Seedcamp.com, or search online for other articles to educate yourself (see also Brad Feld and Jason Mendelson's *Venture Deals*). For now, however, familiarize yourself with these basic terms:

- **"authorized shares"**: Startups incorporate, and the incorporation documents "authorize" a total number of shares (e.g., 10 million), the legal limit on the number of shares an organization is allowed to issue to founders, junior founders, advisors, strategic partners and employees. The number of authorized shares is a somewhat arbitrarily chosen number. For example, if you have 5 authorized shares, then at maximum, you could have 5 owners who each own 20% of the company. But if you choose to authorize a far greater number of shares, you allow there to be more equity stakeholders and for each share to represent a smaller fraction of the company. If you run out of shares, authorizing more is a relatively simple legal process (though with some costs).

- **"angel", "pre-seed", "seed", or "Series A" round:** These terms signal successive stages of the startup. They also correlate with levels of investor sophistication, the size of the investment (relative to the company's worth) and the closeness of personal connections involved in the financing. Homan Yuen, the founder of Solar Junction, currently runs his own venture capital firm. As Homan says, *"These definitions are constantly shifting. An angel round might amount to US$100,000 from friends and family. A seed round anywhere from $200,000-500,000 or US$1-3 million from friends and family and perhaps more sophisticated investors. A Series A round might be US$5-10 million from VC firms. It depends on the industry and the market."*

- **"priced round" versus "convertible note":** The two primary ways to raise investor funds are through a priced round or a convertible note. A convertible note is a loan (principal and interest) that is never intended to be paid back but converts into stock at a future date, based on some yet-to-be-determined price. In this way an investor can loan money to a startup, but instead of getting a return in the form of principal plus interest, the investor receives equity in the company. If the company goes bankrupt, then the investor loses her money. A convertible note may also come with a "discount" or "valuation cap."

In contrast to a convertible note, in a priced round, the startup company will give away equity based on a valuation of the company (where an investor gets a certain number of shares at a price/share). This means you must know (or at least agree upon) the value of the company at the time of the investment, which can be difficult to determine for many early-stage ventures. Raising funds through priced rounds may be slower and more expensive than through convertible notes because the legal and accounting requirements are more complex. Note that there's a raging debate about whether it is better for a startup to raise funds through a priced round or a convertible note.

- **"valuation":** The valuation or value of a company is an imprecise, negotiated assessment of how much your startup is worth. It is based on what investors are willing to pay and what you think investors should pay. It is a *subjective* number! You might think your valuation should be higher than what an investor will agree to. In this case, you may not be willing to sell a portion of your company to this investor, and the investor may not be willing to pay an amount based on your higher valuation.

It's your job to persuade others that your company is worth more than they first think. You might benchmark your startup's valuation against similar companies. But if your company is not earning revenue yet and if there is no competitor or company similar to your company, consider a myriad of other factors to bolster your case for a higher valuation. Note the caliber of the team, the quality of early investors, partners, or supporters, forms of market traction, and expected market size. When valuation becomes critical, talk to your advisors and do an online search for more in depth advice.

- **"term sheet":** This is an investor's written expression of interest in making an investment. It is a mostly non-binding letter of intent (in bullet point or table form) setting forth the basic terms and conditions under which an investment will be made. It will serve as a template to develop the more detailed legal documents. You want to get these written expressions of interest, because until then, it's all just talk and meetings. When you get a term sheet, things are getting real.

- **"vesting schedule"***:* This is a timetable for when one earns allocated shares. That is, ownership of the stock issued to the founders is earned over time (typically four years), rather than owned outright immediately. Vesting schedules protect the company when a founder, co-founder, or critical hire departs the startup (voluntarily or involuntarily) after a few months. The departing person won't hold enough equity to make things like fundraising and decision-making difficult for those who remain.

- **"option pool"**: This is the number of shares allocated for distribution to employees, so that if the company goes public, employees can be compensated with stock.

- **"pre-money" versus "post-money" valuation***:* This represents how much the company is worth at a given point of time: either before or after an investment is made (Pre-money Valuation + Investment = Post-money Valuation). For example, a US$1 million investment in a company valued at US$5 million means you own 1/5th of the company at a pre-money valuation or 1/6th of the company at a post-money valuation.

Once you have some familiarity with finance terms, you'll be on better footing to engage with investors.

Tip #60: Build an Investor Prospect List

You'll need to build a list of potential investors. Use a spreadsheet to keep the list organized. (Nonprofits will use a similar process and prepare a donor prospect list of corporate and family foundations, high net worth individuals, and governmental grant-making organizations.)

1. **Prepare your investor list.** First, draw up a prospect list of angel investors, angel investor groups, and early stage venture capital firms. Venture capital firm and angel fund information is surprisingly available.

    *   *Try AngelList.com and Crunchbase.com*, which have databases of investors and companies. Search the databases for firms investing in your startup space.

    *   *Identify early stage venture capital firms or angel funds in your city.* Simply Google these firms and funds or investor circles, and generate a beginning list. (Angelcapitalassociation.org is also a good place to start.)

    *   *Look for investors that are part of the startup community.* Note which investors are serving on panels or speaking at startup or industry conferences. Pay attention to individuals who seem to offer themselves as resources to young founders, and avoid those who are either very deal focused or too busy to deal with early stage startups. Some venture capital partners have blogs that signal their willingness to be engaged.

    *   *Check out angel investor award lists.* For example, the New England Venture Capital Association, the Angel Capital Association, and TechCrunch give awards to investors, including angel investors.

    *   *Finally, ask friends and contacts for recommendations of potential contacts.* Ask them if they know of investors, firms, or angels that would be interested in your startup and whether they would be willing to make an introduction.

2. **Develop "investor fit profiles" once you have a starter list.** To make sure that there is a good match between your organization and some firm, research the firm's funding objectives to make sure it qualifies as investor. Figure out whether and why they would be interested in investing in you.

- What is the size of the fund? The size of the check will be proportional to the size of the fund.

- What stage companies do they invest in – pre-revenue, pre-product, post-revenue, profitable, unprofitable, or Series A, B, or C companies? Find out where they invest along that spectrum to make sure you're a match for them.

- Finally, what sectors do the firm and the individual partner tend to invest in?

This research will tell you whether they care about your startup's industry space and whether they enjoy investing in startups in general. Their recent investments will also give an indication of the types of companies that currently excite them. (Nonprofits will need to take a similar approach and identify which funding organizations have objectives that most closely align with their mission and stage of operation.)

3. **Engage early and build your potential investor network first.** Fundraising is a process that takes several months of cultivation before your first investors (or donors) actually write a check. Seek their wisdom about how to make your startup grow, ask them for contacts, and learn about their investing preferences before you start fundraising. Also, share your plans for the upcoming months, and update them when you've carried those plans out. Find reasons to continue to engage them. If they continue to be interested in your startup, then when you decide to fundraise, you can reach out to everyone in your investor network, tell them that you are raising money now, and meet them all very quickly.

    Get to know investors over time and before you set out to fundraise. By doing so, you give investors an opportunity to get involved and provide input into a startup that they will want to invest in. (*See also Tip #34 about the importance of cultivating relationships, including before making a big ask.*)

4. **Seek an angel investor to be an anchor.** Look for your first angel investor among those with whom you are already closely connected. This might be a close advisor that you ask to become your first investor before you seek institutional funds. If you have already cultivated a relationship, then you can tell her of your fundraising plans and say that you would be honored if she would

consider being one of your first angels. (Possibly you will offer her a discount on investing in your startup). Your startup will need an anchor (or two) so you can demonstrate that people have already put skin in the game.

Once you have a sufficient list of prospects that have identified, how will you engage them? Have you thought about how much to ask for and why? To be effective at fundraising, you'll need to "know thyself" and be able to justify your fundraising goals.

PRO TIP:

Professional fundraisers know that "when you ask for money you get advice, and when you ask for advice, you get money." People give when they've been part of the consultation and development process. Make sure to engage early and as much as possible before making a financial ask.

Tip #61: Assess Your Startup Fundraising Needs

For-profit and nonprofit startups follow a similar process of preparation (drawing up a donor or investor prospects list; assessing how much to raise in total and how much to ask from each potential prospect and proceeding through a "cultivation," "solicitation," and "stewardship" process that usually takes 12 to 18 months and that leads to a "memorandum of understanding" (in the nonprofit space) or a "term sheet" (in the for-profit space).

1. **First, know when to raise funds.** If you don't need the cash, give yourself time to focus on operations and increase the value of the company, since raising money after you've achieved some milestones will require you to give away less equity for each dollar you raise. Note also that fundraising activities often involve a tradeoff with operational activities. Seek to raise outside funds when:

    - you have made a product and can sell that product repeatedly
    - you believe the company should exist and the bottleneck is the cash
    - the business requires rapid growth (it's not a lifestyle business)
    - you see big potential to scale (institutional investors want scale, because it promises better returns, such as at least a $500 million dollar market)
    - you have just completed or are about to complete a key milestone (investors and potential partners feel less risk at such times)
    - it'll be relatively easy to fundraise (investors are interested in your startup)

2. **Second, know how much you need to fundraise.** Don't fundraise without knowing precisely how the money will be used. To be effective at fundraising, you must have a compelling reason for raising each round of funds (which is also sometimes called a "tranche" of funding). Carefully determine how much cash your startup will need to reach several critical, well-paced milestones.

Do not rush this process. If you are not clear on how the funds will be used and how they further validate your startup idea, you won't be able to convince investors to fund your startup.

- *Break down your biggest goal into discrete levels of progress (not necessarily chronological), and identify how much capital you will need to reach each level.* What salaries will you have to pay yourself and staff, and what other expenditures will help you reach each milestone? You can consider your own salary, whether it is US$30,000 or up to six-figures, as part of your operating cost, since your inability to pay personal bills would negatively impact your productivity.

  While you should not use your salary to enrich yourself, the more money you raise, the more money it is reasonable to allocate to your salary. In addition, figure out your current and projected "burn rate" (the cash used per month) to reach each progress level. Triangulate costs by asking other startups how much time, labor and money were required to build, market test, and validate a product or service like yours.

- *Consider how each milestone represents a meaningful proof point.* Although these vary by industry, here are three primary milestones that you might raise funds to reach:

  (i)   the prototype stage (having a product that is ready to be tested and refined and eventually launched)

  (ii) the revenue generating stage (obtaining your first paying customer)

  (iii) the profit generating stage (selling repeatedly to get your company into the black).

3. **Next, set a fundraising goal. You will fundraise in tranches – for one milestone at a time, so tie your goal to the costs associated with reaching the next one.** This may feel uncomfortable, since you will want to cover as much of your future activities as you can. But investors want to know that their funds are tied to a specific outcome, which validates the startup idea. They also like to make small, initial investments that allow them to test out your startup. When pitching to potential supporters, talk about the milestones that you've achieved thus far and how new support will help you reach the next milestone.

For example, when Michael Schmidt of Vaska Technologies approached potential investors, he told them he had a retail company willing to distribute appliances using his technology in consumers' homes, and he explained that he was raising funds to manufacture the pilot machines so he could get user feedback. By describing exactly how the funds would be used, he was able to fundraise effectively.

4. **Set a timeline for your fundraising goal.** To create a sense of urgency, impose a deadline for raising each tranche, and have a rationale for that deadline. It's okay for the deadline to start loose and then firm up as you gain traction. (For example, at the beginning of the fundraising stage you may tell potential investors that your deadline is "end of summer." As you approach the end of summer and continue to fundraise, you might say that your deadline is September 15th).

Tying specific amounts of money to specific outcomes within a certain time frame is critical to effective fundraising. Once that's done, all you need to do is ask. But how much to ask for?

Tip #62: Assess Asking Amounts

Once you know how much you need to raise to reach the next milestone, you need to know how much someone can invest. If you ask for too little, you will have wasted an opportunity, but if you ask for too much, you might scare off the prospect. (The same considerations apply for nonprofit startups. You will need to assess appropriate asking amounts of donors or other funding sources.)

1. **Gauge someone's "investible funds."** What is the range of investment that a prospect might be comfortable with (four figures? five figures? more?) and how much can a prospect actually afford to invest (her total budget of "investable funds")? This should be an amount that, if lost, does not damage the investor (especially for angel investors).

2. **Use these techniques to assess potential asking amounts**. Explicitly inquire about and do research on what amounts might be within the reasonable range of the prospect:

   - Find articles online that discuss a prospect's past charitable or investment activities.

   - Ask someone who is familiar with the prospect to advise you on an appropriate amount.

   - Ask your prospects explicitly: *"How much have your investments been in the past?"* or *"How much are you thinking about investing in this industry?"* or *"How much are you comfortable investing?"*

   - State the approximate size of other investments in your startup, or state that your startup seeks investments in certain increments, such as *"$50,000 and $100,000 blocks"* or *"in the five to six figure range."* This gives the investor an indicator of the size of the investments you are hoping for.

   - Give more specific boundaries by saying something like, *"Our startup is looking to raise approximately US$100,000 among 3-5 investors"* (this will hint at the size of an investment while preserving significant flexibility).

To make sure you leave the door open, indicate your flexibility if a different amount feels more appropriate or realistic to the investor herself.

3. **As a responsible fundraiser, inform investors that the investment carries some risk.** You will certainly want to frame the investment as an opportunity for the investor – to participate in a possibly lucrative business, to get in early with an equity stake, to work together to leverage each other's businesses in mutually beneficial ways or to be a leader in some domain. But don't hide the fact that any investment carries some risk. Besides being honest, this can assuage own anxieties about taking other people's money.

   If you believe that your startup needs the funds, and if you believe that losing the investment won't damage the investor (who is anyhow aware of the risk), then you have no reason to feel uncomfortable about asking for and accepting an investment.

Once you meet your milestone, go back to your investors and update them about how their funds enabled you to reach your goal. This paves the way for the next round of fundraising. The fundraising process is your responsibility to manage and to make sure it moves at an adequate clip.

Tip #63: Use a Four-Steps-or-Fewer Fundraising Process

New founders often get tripped up on the fundraising process. They have no experience, and they don't know how to follow-up properly or close a deal. You will need to experiment a bit, until you figure out what works for you. (*See Tip #16 on moving from a pitch to a process.*) In general, however, once you have an anchor angel investor and have cultivated a few prospective-investor relationships, it should take four steps or fewer to close.

1. **The four-step fundraising process should look something like the below.** Importantly, the fundraising process is a process – it should follow a predictable pattern that yields somewhat reliable results. (See Tip #16 on moving from a pitch to a process.) Note that this tip assumes you have already cultivated a network of potential investors, you know why you need the funds to reach what milestones, and you have decided to go "all out" to fundraise.

    *   *Step 1: Send out a short email.* Describe directly and openly why you are reaching out, explain briefly why you think there might be a good fit, and conclude by asking something like, "*If this might be a good fit, would you care to talk?*" If they say yes, set up a brief call or meeting. (*See also Tip#18 on how to write short, effective emails that get a response.*)

    *   *Step 2: Screening call or meeting (25 minutes).* The goal of this call is not to pitch the startup but to *confirm* investor interest and aligned objectives, and to get them excited about learning more about the startup. It is also about ensuring they are a good fit for you. At the outset of the call or meeting, state your objective clearly. For example, you can say, "*I was hoping to have a high level conversation where we can share what we are both working on and determine the best way to connect from here. Does that sound good?*" During the conversation, learn more about their investment approach: When do they get involved with companies, what areas are they most interested in getting involved in, what do they enjoy spending their time on, and are they currently invested in companies similar to your startup?

If they are strongly interested in the startup, say something like this: "*It sounds like you're interested and what we're working on is aligned with your goals. We're also selective about who we work with. Given that you are excited at a high level, I'd be glad to continue the conversation.*" If they want to continue the conversation, set up a next meeting.

- *Step 3: Meeting the team.* At this stage, you (and they) have passed the screening stage. Now you will more formally deliver your pitch. The investor will learn more details and meet some members of your team. Continue to gauge their excitement, and continue to learn what you can about their investing style. If the meeting goes well and both parties continue to be excited, reiterate your fundraising plans and ask about their decision-making process and timeline and whether they need you to furnish additional information.

- *Step 4: Due diligence.* At this stage, the investor will be evaluating you and seeking clarification on a number of issues: the team, the market size, the product roadmap, the sales pipeline, the industry, regulatory risk, and the competition. You may begin to discuss deal structure and terms. This due diligence process should lead to the offer of a term sheet.

2. **The goal of the fundraising process is to obtain a term sheet!** An investor will make a funding offer by presenting a term sheet, which is the first concrete step toward money being deposited in your account. If an investor offers the full amount the company thinks it needs – on terms acceptable to the company – then definitive legal paperwork is assembled and signed, the money is wired (or the check is cut), and the round is "closed." If the investor only puts in a portion of the money needed, the startup has a "round in progress" with a "lead investor," and the startup will seek out other investors to invest on the same terms (so there will be multiple signatories to the same term sheet). While investors usually furnish the term sheet, you can also find draft documents, such as YCombinator.com's Simple Agreement for Future Equity (SAFE). Note that angel term sheets tend to be simpler than VC term sheets.

3. **Pitch term sheets against each other.** Fish for term sheets from different investors, so you can choose the one that offers the most

favorable terms or leverage one term sheet in negotiation with another investor. For example, Elad Shoushan is the founder of LTG Exam Prep Platform, an education technology company that offers exam prep programs for phones and tablets. When he tried to raise Series A funding, he calculated a US$3 million need, but quickly got rejected. As Elad says, *"The investors thought our calculated need was too high and unnecessary to reach the milestones. When we adjusted our ask to US$1-2 million, however, we quickly got two term sheets and buy-in from investors. We leveraged those offers to signal to other investors that they should jump on the bandwagon, and we ended up picking the offer with the higher valuation and comparatively favorable terms."*

4. **Take "smart money" from investors who can help you most.** Importantly, when considering whom you want to invite to become an investor in your startup, consider those who will make the best partners. They should celebrate successes with you, help you thrive, make valuable introductions for you, and advise you well. You and your funders enter into a relationship, and you want to enter one that is as positive and mutually beneficial as possible.

Even if you know you need to follow and manage the fundraising process, how do you best ensure that you effectively speak to investor objectives?

THE HOLY GRAIL: A TERM SHEET

When it comes to seeking major commitments, including commitments of money, the goal is the same: a term sheet (or in nonprofit contexts, a "memorandum of understanding", "commitment letter", or "letter of intent"). These documents are not official documents, but they serve the critical function of recording preliminary agreements and signaling that commitment will be forthcoming.

Tip #64: Identify Your Audience and What's in it for Them

Young founders, in their excitement for their startup, often energetically discuss the good that it does for the customer or the world without thinking about the good it does for the specific audience before them. As a result, they miss an opportunity to connect with potential investors (or partners) on the issues that matter most to them. Before you propose an investment or partnership, clearly understand "what is in it for them" to purchase your product, or to partner or invest in your startup.

1. **Correctly identify your audience.** Founders often confuse three categories of people. It's important to keep these three categories distinct in your mind, because they have different interests and perspectives. These categories are:

    *   the *beneficiary* of the product or service
    *   the *purchaser* of the product or service
    *   the *investor* in the startup

    For example, Bailey Ernstes is the CEO of MonitorMed Solutions, a company that is developing an implanted medical hydrocephalus device. This device measures brain pressure and delivers the data to a mobile app, so patients know how effectively their shunt is draining excess fluid in the brain. Originally, Bailey and her team touted the value of the device solely from a patient (or beneficiary) perspective during investor meetings. She talked about how hydrocephalus could be life-threatening to the patient and how patients needed a better way to anticipate a malfunctioning shunt.

    She didn't, however, adequately address investors' concerns about the moneymaking potential of the device, nor did she convince them that she had a good understanding of the market and marketing strategy. At her next investor meeting, however, she focused her pitch on hospitals (the purchasers) rather than patients and discussed how the device would save hospitals money by reducing unnecessary emergency room visits. She also detailed a marketing strategy specifically to reach physicians and neurosurgeons, who significantly influence hospitals' procurement decisions. Since many hospitals would find such cost-savings valuable, demand for the device would be great and investors would stand to benefit financially. Investors received these pitches much more favorably.

Always consider who the beneficiaries, purchasers, and investors are, so you can speak directly to their interests.

2. **Consider your audience's interest at both institutional and individual levels.** For example, Liz Kwo is the co-founder of New Pathways Education and Technology Group, a company that helps Chinese students obtain placements at US high schools and colleges. In meetings with US high schools, she asks explicitly whether the school wants more applicants, more top students, more diversity in their applicant pool, or students who will be beneficial to their existing students in some particular way. She also tries to figure out whether her contact at a school may benefit from the partnership. (An admissions officer might want to show that the school has been receiving a record number of applications.) This attentiveness to both institutional and individual interests maximizes the partnership's benefits for all parties.

3. **All pitches should explicitly address what the other party gets out of the relationship.** You can even send out your prepared notes 10 or 15 minutes before the meeting, and include what's in it for them. You want potential partners to zero in on their interests during the meeting. This tip presumes that you've gone through the necessary steps of cultivating relationships and understanding your counterparts' concerns and interests. (*See Tip #34 about cultivating relationships.*)

In some instances, you'll want to trade favors explicitly, telling others what you can or will do for them in return for their assistance, time, donation or investment. Even if someone hasn't asked for anything in return, you can tack on a sentence like, "*Please tell me if I can ever be of help to you.*" It might feel transactional, but people greatly appreciate your permission, and even invitation, for them to impose on you.

Although you'll do your best to argue for why your startup idea has upside potential and how investors or others will benefit, you'll undoubtedly encounter skepticism that you'll need to diplomatically address.

Tip #65: Ninja Kick Skepticism

Whenever you are trying to do something new or innovative, you will meet skepticism. This is a natural consequence of being on the cutting edge. So you should never expect even your best pitch to find total approval and enthusiasm. Don't be rattled or discouraged when potential supporters express concerns about your startup, and definitely don't take it personally. (*See also Tip #57 about going for low-hanging fruit and those who are already nodding and interested in your startup.*)

Here are some techniques for addressing skepticism clearly and convincingly:

1. **Address objections with specific data.** Rather than relying on opinions or anecdotes, use as much data as you can to refute skepticism. Acknowledge the apparent force of a critique, and then invoke your own "surprise" about this newfound data: "*We were also concerned about this issue, but were surprised to learn that [explain how new data counteracts or refutes the skepticism].*" This expression of surprise conveys humility, rather than arrogance, if your tone is right. Use this approach even if you've heard the same concerns before and are more than ready to defend your startup against these concerns.

2. **Preemptively unveil risks and your strategies to address them:** Don't cover the risk. Do the exact opposite. Tell people "*here's my business, here's what we're doing. Here's how we'll fail if these three things don't happen, so here's how we're addressing them.*" More impressive.

3. **Sell the future by analogizing to the past.** In other words, position your startup as similar in a specific way to a successful company. For example, Senthil Balasubramanian is the co-founder of Sistine Solar, which sells aesthetic coverings that integrate into solar panels. Initially, Senthil would tell investors that he envisioned a world in which design made solar panels so appealing that they would be used everywhere. Investors didn't buy it. They were skeptical about whether the company was scalable and thought it might make a merely niche product. It didn't help that the founding team was comprised of students and first-time entrepreneurs. But when Senthil started to analogize

their product to the iPhone and Tesla electric cars, claiming that Sistine Solar was similarly dealing in an innovative technology where beautiful design and intelligent engineering would spur consumer demand, Sistine Solar obtained its first tranche of funding. Find successful companies who had to overcome similar challenges to those your startup faces, and remind your potential investors that skepticism can be misplaced.

4. **Sell the tenacity and flexibility of the team even if the business model is uncertain.** Funders fund people. Even if you're still validating market interest in your startup's product, ask investors, *"Can you see yourself backing a team that is hungry, desperate to succeed, and keeps hitting its milestones?"*

    For example, Senthil would update potential investors on milestones every few months: how they produced a prototype aesthetic covering; how they got their first paying customers such as Microsoft Corporation and Starwood Hotels and Resorts; and how they closed their seed round of financing. Although certain investors had declined to participate in the first round of funding, in the next fundraising round, Senthil asked if they would back a team that had demonstrated its ability to remain flexible, solve problems, make pivots, and proactively seek a market, even if the business model was not fully validated yet. This time, the investors said yes.

5. **Share your mistakes (and say what you did differently).** Don't recoil from your mistakes. Instead share them and show potential investors what you are now doing differently based on what you learned. People are compelled by narratives of how you discovered a mistake, learned from it, and took a different and successful approach. If you don't tell them such stories, they won't appreciate the process you went through.

    For example, Senthil told investors how his startup's initial strategy to target bus shelters and kiosks turned out not to make a viable market for the solar panel coverings: they learned that it would take too long to get the relevant city permits. However, as a result, they turned to the residential market, since homebuilders had consistently expressed interest. Young founders often hesitate to share their mistakes, but mistakes can add to your credibility when you overcome them. People will admire your responsiveness to new information.

6. **Kill skepticism with a sense of urgency.** For example, investors usually view retail as a "long sell cycle industry" since retailers are generally slow to adopt new technology. Olga Kotsur, of Mercaux, recognized the challenge in getting retailers to adopt her company's technology, but she also argued to investors that she would not need to convert all retailers. Like Senthil, she analogized to the past. Her idea was like e-commerce, she argued, an idea that was mocked at first. Investors that got in early to support e-commerce technology reaped great benefits, while investors that lagged behind missed out. Importantly, Olga emphasized that if retailers *were already ready* to convert to the new technology, then the investor would be *too late to invest*. This reasoning won over her investors and landed her a first round of funding.

7. **Don't be too humble or self-deprecating.** Chase Garbarino founded BostonInno, a local media platform that serves as a mix between traditional news source and corporate pages. He successfully sold his company to a larger media company, but not before he learned to strike a balance between being confident and humble. As Chase shared, *"In investor pitches, I was a little too humble. I would say I didn't know some things, that I needed to work on certain areas more, and that we could get better in these other areas. I was too self-critical and did not give investors confidence."* You still need to sell the dream. Rather than wearing your anxieties on your sleeve, use mentors and advisors to tell you the areas where you can be confident and how to present weaknesses in a way that reassures, but does not mislead, investors.

8. **Articulate as many "proof points" as possible to make a case for why you are investible.** For example, Michael Lisovetsky is the founder of Homeswipe, a rental listing app *"that's more high quality than Craigslist but less onerous than Streeteasy."* As he says, *"In investor meetings, I would list a bunch of marks of approval: how I had a technical person on the founding team, how I was going after a market that is big, how our team kept hitting milestones, how we were accepted into an accelerator program, and how we had early support from Tim Draper."* You can similarly laundry list your proof points. Use the word "proof" and show investors that:

- you can attract a team and work together as a team
- you can build a working prototype (product development)
- you can obtain first users and clients (product launch)
- you can talk to investors (first financing, even if small)
- you can talk to audiences (many users or subscribers)
- you can attract talent (first key hire at the C-suite or VP level)
- respected industry advisors or partners are on board
- you can capture a market (e.g., sales of $1M annually)
- you can manage your finances (e.g., cash-flow positive)
- you can scale (e.g., sales of $10M annually)
- the market is big! (e.g., sales of $25M annually and beyond)

When you need to show that you are you're worthy of investment, these techniques will help you make a persuasive case. Once you do, follow-up!

NINJA MOVES FOR NAYSAYERS:

Overcome skepticism of your startup idea with these easy moves:

1) Sell the future by analogizing to the past.

2) Sell the tenacity and flexibility of the team (even if the business model is uncertain).

3) Share your mistakes (and say what you did differently).

Tip #66: Follow-up on Investor Meetings Effectively

Let's say you've reached out to a number of prospects and had meetings. How do you get these parties to commit to your startup? How should you follow up? How aggressively you follow up on an investor meeting will naturally depend on how conversations have gone, how well you know the investor and how far along your startup is. If you have already carefully assessed your startup needs, are convinced that you need outside funds to reach the next compelling milestone, have a track record of success (e.g., hitting your milestones) and you think there is a good investor fit, then the decision to fundraise means you should be working quickly to get commitments. These tips also apply to donors and other funding agencies. (See also Jeffrey Bussgang's *Mastering the VC Game*.)

1. **Demand clarity and transparency on the fundraising process.** You are in control of and responsible for managing your fundraising. Ask who is the decision-maker and about the process of decision-making, and sequence the fundraising process. Proactively engage, feed updates, and find out the conditions for mutual levels of commitment. For example, ask, "*If I hit x milestones, what will you do? Does it hit your bar such that you will make the next level of commitment? If not, what do you need to see?*" Also ask permission to send additional documents or to come back in a few weeks.

2. **Never leave a meeting with investors without asking what happens next.** At the conclusion of the investor meeting, ask questions like:

   - What more do they need in order to decide?
   - Do they need another meeting with you?
   - What do they want to talk about, and how soon?
   - Do they need to do something internally, like talk to their partners or investigate a certain issue? How long do they expect it to take?
   - What issues are still outstanding for them, and is there any information you can provide?

Feel free to justify your questions by saying that you're not sure how the fundraising process works. You need to know where you stand – don't let yourself be in limbo land! If investors don't answer such questions, assume they aren't interested.

3. **Create a real (not faux) competitive dynamic and convey a sense of urgency.** Find an actual alternative, be in a situation where you are cash flow break even, or have an angel, or can just operate without additional funds, or be in talks with two or three great firms. Create real choices for yourself. Convey the sense of urgency and say, "*We're in a lot of meetings. I'm not able to say with whom, but we're in a lot of conversations, and one or two have expressed interest.*" VCs like to buy time, because they can see more proof points and minimize their risk. Entrepreneurs, however, need to make decisions and move fast.

4. **Figure out if you're still cultivating or under actual consideration.** Observe behavior: Are they setting up meetings, exposing you to partners, asking you for bios, or calling your references? They are generating the energy and following up. Don't confuse politeness for interest. Partnerships and organizations are structured differently. Your deal champion may love your startup idea, but if all members of the partnership must agree to make and investment and you're not meeting the whole partnership, then you're not in an investment process. Ask: "*Am I one of the two or three most important new deals you're working on right now?*" Given the limited number of investments that any one firm might make, if the answer is no, then you are not really in an investment process.

5. **Follow-up directly and quickly.** New entrepreneurs aren't accustomed to hounding someone for a response. But you need to. For example, if you met with an investor on a Friday, *early the next week* you can reach out to the potential investor and politely say: "*I wanted to check in with you about your decision. What I'd like to do is set up a call before the end of the week so we know where you stand. We have a few other investors in the pipeline. It won't take long. We just want to see how things are going.*" Being persistent and following-up promptly convey a sense of urgency and add the appearance of value to your startup.

If they end up not investing, then, in three months, you should follow-up with an update. Say: "*Hi, I just wanted to let you know that we accomplished these milestones, we raised this amount and still have an open round, so we wanted to check in with you.*" Or "*I know last time you weren't interested, but we have new developments and I'd like to follow up with a short call if you are free this week.*" If no one responds, you should follow-up with the contact, the secretary, or a junior partner. Get closure on where the party stands.

6. **Do not be afraid to push for the No.** Nos are going to happen. You will encounter many Nos before you get to a Yes. You will need the Nos so you can move on to actual prospects. Sara Gragnolati is the founder of Cocomama. She started her company as she was looking for her own gluten-free options and couldn't find any to her satisfaction. Looking back on her fundraising experience, she says, "*In the beginning, I allowed people to stay in the I'm-interested-in-you-I-want-to-see-what-happens-to-you category for too long. I should have forced them to make a decision, because I had to spend a lot of time talking with people who weren't going to write more than a US$10,000 or US$25,000 check. Now, I'm not afraid to force a decision. I follow up every day. I don't wait a week and I'm not afraid to pick up the phone. I say, 'We're closing the round soon.' I ask, 'Where are we at?', 'What else do you need?', or 'Is this something you want?' You just have to get an answer.*"

GO FOR THE NO ... TO GET TO THE YES!

Nos are going to happen. Welcome them because they will lead you to those who are excited about what you're doing. Don't let people dilly dally on getting back to you. Assertively push for an answer so you can move on to prospects who can say yes to you.

Tip #67: Make a Mindset Shift – You Have Something to Give

In the entrepreneurial process, you will often feel like the supplicant: you are constantly out on the road, lining up meetings, asking for connections or favors or seeking funds for your startup. Making a big ask can also feel high-stakes, because you may be rejected and because any investment entails some risk to the investor. For social entrepreneurs or those working on nonprofit startups, asking for donations may be even more difficult, because the investor does not receive a financial stake.

To overcome this discomfort, shift your mindset and stop seeing yourself as a supplicant. Even at your startup's nascent stages, you are someone who has **something worthwhile to offer** others:

1. **You're *giving*, not taking.** When you raise funds, view yourself as *giving* others an opportunity to get involved in a meaningful initiative or to benefit from a new and successful business. This mindset shift will be easy to make if you have convinced yourself already of the value of what you're doing (meeting an "unmet need"), and if you have thought through what you have to offer to others ("what's in it for them").

    Moreover, if you've cultivated a relationship with your contact and adequately researched your prospect's financial situation to the extent possible, then you should feel confident that an investment or partnership is beneficial to both parties. You'll understand what would be an appropriate type and size of ask, and understand that any risks are manageable and worth bearing. If you find yourself unconvinced, then you need to take more time to assess how your startup aligns with the needs and interests of the other party.

2. **You're a northbound train.** Not only should you be confident that you have something worthwhile to offer, you should feel certain you'll get what you want, regardless of who gives it to you. If you believe that you will get to where you're headed and that others can either join you or miss out on a great opportunity, then you'll be able to stay calm and confident in meetings. Intentionally cultivate this outcome-independent mindset and project this confidence in pitch meetings.

3. **Remember, what you're searching for is also searching for you.** Investors don't want to sort through tons of ideas. They are looking for good people that they can work with and good ideas that they can invest in. They want to find you as much as you want to find them. If you offer true value in a partnership, then you can assume someone will be interested in investing, and your conversation will feel natural rather than forced.

Make sure that you have fully adopted this mindset shift: You have something valuable to offer to the other party, and you are an unstoppable northbound train merely making a stop at some particular meeting, where you expect to take on passengers before you roar away.

This mindset, in conjunction with a high level of due diligence on the need to fundraise, the expected use of funds, and the strength of investor appetite, should support you well in your fundraising efforts. The next chapter touches upon final considerations for how to hold yourself and the ship steady in a precarious startup climate.

PART NINE

HOW TO KEEP AND CEDE CONTROL

HOW TO KEEP AND CEDE CONTROL

My startup has grown and now involves a lot of people, many of whom are more senior than I am – people such as investors, board members, and advisors. How do I manage my team and myself as my startup continues to grow? How do I maintain my authority, my vision, and my strategic direction when others don't always share my views?

Four intense years into the AWLU Project, one of my senior board members, Judy Cheng-Hopkins, informed me that she would like to be president. At the time, our organization was struggling to obtain a university license from the Malaysian Ministry of Education, and our team was divided on the best way to proceed. One option was to take the issue to the media. Another strategy was to continue working through governmental back channels. Judy was a senior UN official from Malaysia and was well connected to top Malaysian officials and international leaders. She was also articulate, smart and savvy in navigating political processes. Although I struggled immensely with this decision (the AWLU Project was my baby!), Judy's presidency could help us overcome the many political hurdles we had been facing. With these and other factors in mind, I passed on the baton to Judy. Although we didn't obtain the license or ultimately succeed in establishing the AWLU, it was my immense privilege to have worked on the effort. New founders often wonder if the risk and sacrifice and the many years they devote to a startup are worth it. The below tips remind you that even through struggles, the startup journey is valuable indeed.

<figure>∞∞∞</figure>

Tip #68: Expect Conflict

If you were dating someone, would you expect to agree all the time? Probably not. Similarly, don't be naïve about the startup process and believe that you'll be able to avoid conflict entirely. In any setting where multiple people are working together, when work can be stressful and stakes feel high, personalities and ideas will sometimes clash.

1. **The more successful your startup becomes, the more conflict you can expect.** Whether they are board members, co-founders, partners, or employees, stakeholders will battle over power, influence, resources, decisions, and the perceived spoils of the startup, even before there are any profits. Competing factions may emerge, and one or another faction may even seek to dislodge you from your position as leader.

    If the division becomes wide enough, the startup risks splitting up (just like in dating, not all relationships are meant to last). Don't fight the inevitable, but do emphasize how each team member provides complementary and essential skills and how you all need each other to succeed. Ask how you can better support each other's work, and remind people to make decisions in the best interests of the startup. Remind them that the startup's ultimate success will lead to individual success, too. (*See also Tip #36 on building a stakeholder interest with your key partners*).

2. **Recognize the tradeoff between collaboration and control.** Whenever you collaborate with others, whether they are employees, investors, board members, or key clients, you inevitably give up some control. When you invite someone to join the board, you cede some of your authority to that person, and even if you have a majority of the equity and voting power, you may still be subject to your board members' views. After all, you probably want to maintain their level of involvement or investment. One board member's dissatisfaction can also cause other board members to depart. And no matter how carefully you choose your initial board members, they will have their own ideas and some power. Recognizing this tradeoff is the first step to managing any conflict that arises from it.

3. **Resolve conflicts by agreeing on objective measures.** Startups require many parts to come together, each of which is integral to the success of the whole. Each member who contributes a critical part becomes a critical player, one with effective veto power. When competing views are mutually exclusive but appear equally meritorious, the conflict gets especially sharp. To resolve such conflicts:

    - Refer explicitly to **previously agreed upon common goals** and principles (*See also Tip #26*). Sometimes these get clouded or forgotten during in the conflict, but you can use them to bring parties back to their common ground.
    - Identify **objective ways** to determine which is the most effective way to reach agreed upon goals (refer to existing data, agree to A/B test and make the decision a data-driven one.
    - Find a **neutral third party** whom all parties trust to decide the best course of action and break the impasse.

These measures take egos out of the equation and remind everyone that there is not "my solution" and "your solution"; rather there is just "the best solution" that serves the startup's priorities and goals. And if you know of the best solution, how can you guide others to see the light, especially if there are many people who are all talking but not agreeing?

Tip #69: Steer Meetings and Decisions

As a founder you will naturally feel a deep personal investment in your idea, and you will want to maintain control over the vision and direction of your startup. However, as your startup grows, people on your startup team will have their own ideas, strategies, and priorities, and their views will not always align with your vision. Below are strategies for maintaining your vision and strategic direction, even as you need more agreement by more people to reach a decision.

1. **Grab attention and authority in meetings.** Meetings that include a lot of talking without any clear outcome or decision are frustrating. Call attention to key issues and action items by asking:

   - *"Can we all agree...?"* or
   - *"Can I propose that we...?"*

   These phrases are powerful because you are explicitly calling for people to voice their opinions. They orient attention, ensure that there is shared understanding on key principles or next steps and move conversations from dialogue to agreement. They also allow you to set the strategic direction since you are proposing the next steps that you think everyone should take. As long as some people agree with what you are proposing (even if others remain silent on these questions), you can move ahead. (*See also Tip #39 on facilitating meetings and Tip #40 on fostering collaboration among your team.*)

2. **Announce your plans to carry out some action.** Don't ask for permission for courses of action. Instead signal what you intend to do by using these words: *"I plan to..."* If other members don't object to your announcement at that time, they have essentially waived the right to complain later. Deploy these words frequently. They expand and define your authority, while keeping everyone in the loop. (No one can later claim to have been bypassed or surprised by your actions.) The larger and more senior your team becomes, the more important it will be for you to show respect for other's opinions, even as you exercise your own deserved authority.

3. **Frame how decisions benefit others.** Founders make the decisions they believe serve the interest of the startup, but team

members will have their own interests and motivations in mind. To persuade others, explain how they will personally benefit from following a particular proposal. The more controversial the decision, the more you will need to speak to other's interests to obtain their support. (*See Tip #64 on being aware of your audience and "what's in it for them".*)

4. **Before announcing a major decision, get the buy-in of Top Dogs.** Young founders often pursue the most direct route for decision-making: when a group decision is needed, they gather the people who have decision-making power (such as a board), make a proposal, allow some time for discussion, and then take a vote.

   This approach might seem obviously appropriate, but it is not the most effective way to manage your startup's affairs, because there is a good chance you will not get the outcome you think is best. Board meetings, in particular, are not a place to make decisions, since egos and personal interests often come to the fore. Also, if you have investors on a board, they never want to be surprised. So talk to your "top dogs" first, let them know what's coming and where you stand before convening the decision-making group.

   - *First, identify your Top Dogs.* These are the most important people on your board, the ones with the most stature, influence and respect.
   - *Second, talk with each Top Dog individually.* Ask each of them for feedback on your proposal and make sure they are all in your corner.
   - *Third, present your idea to the group.* Support from the Top Dogs makes it much more likely that your proposal will be adopted or ratified by others.

Use these strategies to shepherd a group of decision-makers and to iron out difficult issues in advance. Note that the more your team is comprised of multifaceted interests, the more politicking will be necessary. This is natural, but note that the requirement for such politicking may foreshadow a future split. Carving out authority is hard enough. Ensuring that you are recognized for the positive outcomes produced under your authority and leadership is another responsibility you'll need to tackle.

Tip #70: Don't Be A Martyr: Claim Credit

Young founders, excited to be working on their startup and grateful for any support they get, are often better at giving credit to others than at claiming credit for themselves. Claiming credit can seem narcissistic, but you must let your accomplishments be known and avoid the martyrdom trap – where individuals give and give of themselves until they are burned out and broke and then let others take most of the credit. Martyrdom here is not a virtue. In fact it will put the welfare of the startup at risk. If you believe your startup will flourish most under your leadership, you must continuously demonstrate your legitimacy as the leader.

Call attention to your accomplishments and contributions in these comfortable and subtle ways:

1. **Claim your founder status at the beginning of the startup.** List this title in your documents and on business cards, even though you may feel sheepish later if your startup eventually folds. Remember that if you succeed, you'll want this credit, and it must be established from the beginning.

2. **Tag on the words "for you" to signal your value to others.** For example, someone might say, *"Can you email Mike and set up a meeting?"* Don't just answer, *"Sure I can."* Instead, say, *"Sure, I can do that for you."* Adding these words emphasizes your value to the person making a request.

3. **Ask permission to carry out uncontroversial actions to remind people of your value.** If you carry out good deeds without asking for approval, your efforts might be taken for granted. Asking for approval for actions that are not controversial, that would obviously be good for the organization, and that you would have done without permission reinforces people's awareness of your initiative, commitment, and contributions. You don't risk giving authority away, because the action itself was never really in question.

4. **"Socialize" your accomplishments.** Good deeds must not go unsung. Provide regular updates about what the team has

accomplished by presenting accomplishments, such as "*Our team accomplished these goals this week...*" (even if you did most or even all of the work). Although you do not say, "*I achieved this,*" or "*I did that,*" you signal your leadership in facilitating those accomplishments.

5.   **Share your sacrificial acts.** It is very likely that you will make personal sacrifices – skip a dinner or an event to meet a critical timeline, use personal resources, or impose on a personal connection – to further the aims of your startup. Make these sacrifices legible to others. For example, you can say, "*I have evening plans tonight, but I can finish early and come back to clean up the document and send it out this evening.*" Don't be shy.

As the startup becomes a true joint effort where others are now convinced of the value of the startup and visibly stand to gain from the startup's success, the startup will carry its own momentum. Paradoxically, at this point, you may need to re-evaluate and assert your own relevance to the enterprise.

Tip #71: Keep Yourself Relevant

As you create an environment in which stakeholders feel respected, and as your official power is diluted by the addition of valuable but potentially headstrong stakeholders such as board members, investors, or key hires, you must also do all you can to maintain your relevance. No one will do this for you. It is your responsibility to do this for yourself. Here's how:

1. **Believe you matter.** You must believe that the startup needs your leadership, entrepreneurial vision, and passion, and that it will continue to benefit from the skills that enabled you to launch the venture in the first place. Take time to bullet point for yourself how you contribute to the startup so you have an accurate assessment of how you contribute to and are valuable to your enterprise.

2. **Establish a norm that you must be consulted.** Without seeming arrogant or entitled, insert – and assert – yourself in decision-making procedures. Participate in all significant conference calls, conversations, meetings and pitches, so that it becomes a norm. If you have to miss one, make sure that people report back to you.

3. **Highlight your association (or perceived association) with high-status, well-respected individuals and groups, both inside and outside of your startup.** Your relationship (or the appearance of a sufficiently strong relationship) with these individuals or groups enhances your own status and signals your access to a key resource. Even perceived connections help to maintain your authority, your relevance, and your leverage with stakeholders.

4. **Maintain personal relationships and regular contact with influential stakeholders.** For example, Ken Fan, of Ad Gene, schedules informal coffee chats with influential members of his organization even during good times. These conversations have helped him build rapport, and they let him know what's on the minds of his key stakeholders. Sometimes he spots potential conflicts before any arise and can head them off. Schedule informal meetings or check-in calls with your Top

Dogs (and other influential team members) even when there are no controversies. Then, when you are in a tough spot, you can consult with these individuals without seeming underhanded.

5. **Diversify your organization with influential stakeholders who are independent of each other.** While ownership and control are critical factors that determine outcomes of decisions, loyalties also drive human behavior. So, don't let too many of the most important people in your startup (directors, key hires, lawyers, advisors) come from the network of a single source (like an investor group).

    While you should of course leverage contacts, you should also make sure you have a real diversity of independent perspectives to turn to. When the stakes are highest, you will need brutal honesty from advisors and counselors whose viewpoints are not clouded by personal loyalties.

The suggestions in this tip hint at the challenges that can arise when others question your authority, judgment, or leadership, or engage in behavior that is not acceptable to you. When such things happen, and they likely will, you'll need to take a deep breath and head off the issue before it becomes unresolvable.

Tip #72: Prepare for Difficult Conversations

The entrepreneurial road is beset with bumps, both large and small. Some of these bumps involve raising difficult issues, confronting others about something that is bothering you, and admitting when something is just not working. It's challenging and uncomfortable to state that things are going awry, that someone is not working hard enough, that the expected outcomes are not being achieved, or that a certain kind of behavior isn't acceptable.

These conversations may feel personal, and they may even lead to breakups. In fact, you should expect that the closer the relationship, the harder the conversation will be. But ignoring a problem is not a good option because problems don't go away on their own. And if they worsen, you will feel more and more frustrated, and you may pass the point at which a correction is possible.

Here is how to address such difficult situations (see also *Difficult Conversations* by Douglas Stone, Bruce Patton, and Sheila Heen):

1. **First, prepare for the conversation with some personal reflection.** What emotions is the situation stirring up for you? What is your hypothesis about the other person's intentions? How might the other person perceive the same situation? Why is this issue important to you? How does it relate to the goals and priorities of the startup? If your concerns are not addressed, what might be the consequences, and are you willing to live with them? You should be able to identify the crux of the issue in one sentence and identify the feelings you are experiencing.

2. **Second, get into a good (positive) emotional state**. If you are composed enough to broach the issue with a level of emotional detachment, you can move to the next step. (*See Tip #46 on being the voice of calm.*)

3. **Third, initiate the difficult conversation.** Invite the other person to talk with you and schedule a time to talk, if it can't happen straight away. In the conversation:

- *Objectively describe the situation.* Stick to the facts, and be as neutral, detached and unemotional as possible. (If you can't do this, you are not yet ready for this conversation.)

- *Subjectively share how you feel.* While doing so, strike a tone of mutual respect so that the conversation does not feel accusatory. Use "I" statements (e.g., "*I felt….*" rather than "*You did…*") so as not to ascribe blame. Acknowledge ways you may have "contributed" to the situation, and be sure to distinguish intent from the impact the person has had on you ("*I know you didn't intend to, but I felt hurt when…*")

- *Encourage the other person to help you understand her point of view.* Adopt a learning stance in which you investigate the other person's perspective. For example, you can say, "*I'm anxious about bringing this up, but at the same time, it's important to me that we talk about it . . . Can you tell me more or help me understand your perspective?*"

- *Repeat back what the other person has said.* Do this to make sure that you understand correctly and also to show that you were listening, that you care about what the other person had to say.

- *Tell the person you value the relationship.* You can say something like "*I really value you and enjoy working with you. That's why I'm bringing this up. I wanted to talk this out with you so I can understand how you're seeing the situation and clear things up with no hard feelings.*" You should say what you want for yourself (expressing yourself as authentically as possible), but also what you want for the other person (taking into account her interests) and what you want for the relationship (acknowledging your intention to preserve the relationship).

- *Finally, clarify next steps by directly requesting what you want of the other party.* Useful language for this is: "*Please don't…*", or "*I need you to….*" This direct request is the critical, yet often the forgotten, part of these difficult conversations. It puts the onus on the other party to honor or to shun the request, the action that will either preserve or sever the relationship.

Discussion like this should lead to a mutual understanding. However, if the person does not respect your request or if you cannot reach an agreement, consider your options, assess the potential impact of each option, and decide what you need to do. Sometimes it is best to part ways before you commit further time and resources to a relationship that is no longer fruitful.

Tip #73: Identify Your Jump-ship Conditions

Vegas is a gamble; so is entrepreneurship. You should not go to Vegas without a notion of how much you are willing to risk. Similarly, before you roll the entrepreneurial dice, determine either (a) *how much* you are willing to lose, or (b) for *how long* you are willing to endure a losing streak. Decide ahead of time on a certain set of conditions that will indicate it's time to jump-ship, exit your startup, and pursue other projects or lines of work. Your decision calculus should assume that pivots have not been fruitful. (*See Tip #15 on not being so stuck to your initial startup idea and being open to pivoting.*)

Your jump-ship conditions also should be based on personal circumstances that include your startup's financial runway, your appetite for risk, your career aspirations, your own interest levels, and your other work opportunities. For example, you might decide to jump ship if:

- your team works at cross purposes or feels distrust and unease
- you don't raise X amount of dollars by the end of the year
- you don't land your first major client by the end of the year
- you can't pilot your product by the end of the year
- you're not meeting the milestones you've laid out
- if you have been feeling ineffective for more than a set amount of time
- you are emotionally spent or no longer having fun
- you would rather spend your time and energy elsewhere or have found a more interesting, exciting, and promising project or career
- personal or financial circumstances require you to do so

Your jump-ship conditions can always be adjusted, but be sure to have some at the outset, and make sure they cover a specific period of time. Having a clear sense of your boundaries will help you to budget the risk you're willing to carry at any particular moment.

TITANIC CHOICES:

Don't be afraid to jump ship if you realize your startup is heading straight toward an iceberg. It's safer to let go, than to drown in, an unsuccessful startup. Keep your "jump ship" conditions clear, just in case it comes time to change directions or start over.

Tip #74: You Can Quit – You're Not a Failure!

Your resilience in the face of obstacles and doubt, and your faith in the startup idea, are essential to your organization. But even these laudable qualities cannot guarantee success. We know that the vast majority of startups will not survive, even with abundant resilience, optimism, and perseverance. The likelihood of "failure" is even greater when it is your first venture. This information is not intended to discourage you, but to provide some perspective in case your startup does not flourish as you had hoped.

1. **A startup is not a life sentence.** If you have been at it for a while and you find that, despite your best efforts, your startup is draining resources, generating ongoing anxiety, making you unhappy, or negatively impacting other areas of your life, *pay attention to those signals*. If your startup is not progressing at a promising rate or it is no longer personally rewarding, you are not required to soldier on forever.

2. **Letting go of your startup takes courage.** You might feel that you have failed or worry about disappointing those who believed in you or who invested in your startup. However, you cannot allow these feelings to keep you from stepping away from your startup if, after considered thought, you decide that letting go is the best choice for you or your family.

    If you have adequately gauged investors' investible funds, provided accurate information, including the natural risks involved in investing in a startup (*see Tip #62*), you have acted responsibly. Investors should be aware of the risks involved and factored them into their investment decision.

    As for the people who believed in you, you will be surprised how many of them are thoroughly understanding and supportive of your decision to step away. These people want what is best for you and they will not be inclined to judge you. Their encouragement of your efforts was rooted in their positive feelings about *you*, not in their appraisal of the startup itself. In any case, like most of us, they are busy with their own lives, and the fate of your startup is hardly the alpha and omega of their existence!

3. **You can always start another startup!** If you enjoyed the entrepreneurial process, you can always try your hand at another one. The next time out, you will be better prepared, and your first attempt, even though you left, will add to your credibility. Most successful entrepreneurs failed in their first ventures.

4. **Define success based on what you learned and how much you benefitted from the experience.** You must reject the pernicious and false idea that *"If my startup doesn't work out, then I'm also a failure."* Instead, focus on what you have gained from your entrepreneurial journey. For example, you will have:

   - Learned how to develop a concept and make an idea come to life
   - Built enduring friendships and networks that you will carry forward
   - Acquired skills in fundraising, product development, leadership, etc.
   - Earned pride from the milestones you reached
   - Gained experience and credibility in launching new initiatives

5. **Leverage your startup experience for your next venture, whatever that may be.** If you want to go to work for someone else's startup, you will be a highly sought after candidate because of your previous entrepreneurial experience. If you return to a job at an established company, your entrepreneurial skills and experience will give you a leg up over those in the company who have not founded their own ventures. And when you are ready to embark on your next startup, your first startup will have served as a strong training ground. Finally, investors like to invest with those who have previous entrepreneurial experience, even if the first venture did not endure. The courage, energy, and dedication that you poured into your first project will make you a stronger and wiser leader of future endeavors.

After four years of dedicated work on the AWLU Project, it was time to let go and move on. When we didn't get the university license we needed and the organization had to close, I felt like I had let down people who believed in it and in the work we were doing, and who had donated money and time. With some perspective, however, I can say that I am grateful for the experience and the privilege of leading such an effort.

The entrepreneurial experience will be one of the greatest learning and growing opportunities of your life – an experience that few will ever have. Whatever happens, enjoy and appreciate the ride.

Tip #75: Take Care of Yourself

Throughout the entrepreneurial process, you must take care of yourself emotionally, socially, financially, and physically in order to maintain your productivity and happiness. Becoming an entrepreneur can be terrifying and hard, especially if you have quit your job or turned down a job offer or burned through your own savings in pursuit of your dream. Prioritize your own health and well being, both mental and physical.

1. **As you step away from a more traditional and secure career path, be prepared to cope with your own anxiety.** Given the unpredictability of entrepreneurial life, a founder's level of confidence can fluctuate a lot. Though friends and family say nothing outright, you may feel they privately believe that you are wasting your time or squandering your potential. You must fight off the temptation to compare yourself to someone on a corporate career track or a more traditional career path, since your startup experience will not be comparable.

2. **Your own health is good for the startup's health.** If you are working by yourself and not in a structured office setting, you can wind up isolated from a lot of social support. In the early days of your startup, you might be working day and night, devoting virtually all of your time and energy to the project. To combat fatigue and social isolation, figure out what makes you feel balanced. Taking breaks, physical exercise, and good nutrition should all be high priorities. Meditation can also be an excellent source of calm, and you should find time to talk to your friends and family! If your own stress is out of control, you will be less likely to make good decisions, manage relationships smoothly, or lead your startup effectively.

3. **Schedule your work, personal, social, and rest periods.** After a year or so, you should be hitting your stride and settling into a reasonable daily pace. Set up a regular schedule that includes both "work time" and "personal time." Define times when you plan to socialize, exercise, or take a break. Even at work, consider color-coding different obligations (like coffee chats, investor meetings, and travel) so you can see how you are allocating your time. If

you schedule social events with friends in the evenings, this will hold you accountable to being productive during the day and to relaxing later.

4. **Create a "care team," a personal council of advisors who are more invested in you than in the startup.** Your support system can include old friends, mentors, or family members. But they should *not* be directly involved with your startup. These are the people to turn to when you run into trouble or when you feel doubt. They are people whom you trust, with whom you can speak openly, and who will have your best interests in mind. Set up regular check-ins and engage in "failure calls" where you share what has not gone well or as ideally as possible. This will let you vent and also help you learn from these experiences. Your care team will want you to succeed at your startup, but they will also know when it might be time for you to move on to other projects.

A good founder is a good caretaker, making sure that others' needs are being met – but don't neglect yourself! Your own physical, mental, and emotional wellness ensure that the startup journey continues to be as meaningful and rewarding as it should be.

Conclusion

I hope you've found this book helpful as you think about the process of launching your startup. You should now understand the fundamental principles and processes of entrepreneurship. You know how to get started, how to work towards your startup goals, and how to recruit founding team members, advisors, and board members.

You should also have a strong sense of how to approach potential customers, partners, and investors. Importantly, you should be aware that fundraising follows a fairly defined process – starting with outreach, cultivation, and qualifying; moving to pitching; and following through to reach a term sheet or a memorandum of understanding.

You also understand the unique responsibilities that you as a founder will bear – to walk a sometimes lonely path, to serve as the moral and practical compass of your organization, to be the face of stability and confidence, and to be the facilitator, the motivator, and the inspirer for the rest of your team.

With small steps, you can tackle these challenges, and we've covered many of them thoroughly in this book – things that every new founder needs to learn. Some will learn more quickly or more intuitively than others, and many founders have had to learn these lessons by a lot of trial and error. But by picking up this book, you have saved yourself a lot of time and needless anxiety and blind experimentation.

I encourage anyone who has an idea about which they are passionate to pursue it, if not for the ultimate realization of the dream, then for the journey itself. I truly hope that my readers come up with ideas and innovations that contribute to human flourishing and that these tips support you on your incredible journey.

Recommended Resources

Here I have compiled a list of resources, websites, and tools, for learning more about and operating within the startup ecosystem. Anytime you come up to a particular challenge, Google search articles and suggested websites, programs, software, extensions, or web platforms that can aid your work.

BOOKS:

1. Sue Wang, *22 Legal Mistakes You Don't Have to Make*

2. Noam Wasserman, *Founder's Dilemma*

3. Jonas Kjellberg, Tom Kosnik, *Gear Up, Lena Ramfelt*

4. Guy Kawasaki, *Art of the Start*

5. Eric Ries, *Lean Startup*

6. Blake Mycoskie, *Start Something That Matters*

7. Peter Drucker, *Five Most Important Questions*

8. Peter Thiel, *Zero to One*

9. Brad Feld and Jason Mendelson, *Venture Deals*

10. Jeffrey Bussgang, *Mastering the VC Game*

11. Oren Klaff, *Pitch Anything*

12. William H. Draper, *Startup Game*

13. Daniel Pink, *To Sell Is Human*

14. Chip & Dan Heath, *Made to Stick*

15. Douglas Stone, Bruce Patton, and Sheila Heen, *Difficult Conversations*

16. Andy Smith and Jennifer Aaker, *Dragon Fly Effect*

17. Alexander Osterwalder and Yves Pigneur, *Business Model Generation*

18. Thomas Eisenmann (editor), *Managing Startups: Best Blog Posts*

WEB-BASED RESOURCES:

Communication: Google Hangout, Skype, Join.Me, Freeconferencecall. com, Hipdial.com, Slack.com, Basecamp.com, mailchimp.com, Buffer. com (to manage social media), Hootsuite, Klout.com, tweetpages.com.

Stock Photos: Istockphoto.com, Shutterstock.com and Depositphotos. com, Picography.co, Unsplash.com, Isorepublic.com.

Startup Communities: StartupGrind.com, Meetup.com, Vencaf. org. See also SeedRankings.com (to learn more about the top startup accelerator programs).

Startup Blogs: Foundrs.com, Crowdfunder.com, YCombinator.com, Venturehacks.com, Bothsidesofthetable.com, Clerky.com, Seedcamp. com. Also see Orrick's Startup Tool Kit (for term sheets and other startup forms).

YouTube Channels: Harvard Innovation Labs, 500 Startups, This Week in Startups, How to Start a Startup, Startup Grind, Techcrunch, Y Combinator, Greylock Partners, Startupfood.

Website Builder: Wordpress.org, Wix.com, Fatcow.com, Squarespace. com, Weebly.com, Hostt.com.

Visuals: PowToon.com, Animoto.com, or Moovly.com (for videos), Infographics.space (to generate infographics), and Slidevana.com (for presentation templates).

Freelancers: Mechanical Turk by Amazon, Upwork.com, Fiverr. com, CrowdFlower.com, Freelancer.com, Spare5.com, Guru.com, CloudFactory.com, EAhelp.com (for executive assistants). Also consider Tradeaway.com (to barter services).

Programs: Streak, Yesware (to monitor email), Any.do (to assist with scheduling) Zendesk (for consumer support), Infusionsoft (for customer relationship management), Hubstaff (to monitor freelancers), Quickbook Cloud (accounting software), Freshbooks (to assist with invoicing and payments), Due.com (to assist with payroll).

Small Business: Score.org, Sba.gov, Healthcare.gov (to learn about health insurance requirements), Department of Labor (to learn about required worker's compensation coverage), Bureau of Labor Statistics (to prepare to hire a new employee), AICPA (to find a CPA).

Health: Happify (to access free games), Sparkpeople.com, myfitnesspal.com (to count calories or log activity), Yogis Anonymous (to access streaming of "live" classes), Calm.com (to access guided meditation).

Startup Lawyers: Startuplawyer.com, Linkilaw.com, UpCounsel. com, Lawtrades.com, LegalZoom.com and Rocketlawyer.com. Also, check out the large law firms that support startup ventures in the Silicon Valley, such as Perkins Coie, Goodwin Proctor, Wilson Sonsini Goodrich & Rosati, or Fenwick and West.

Prototyping: Balsamiq.com, InVisionapp.com, Autocad, Justinmind, UXPin, Marvel App.

Media: Medium.com (to publish your own content), huffingtonpost. com (to be a guest blogger), Google Alerts, Inc.com (to track news alerts on your company, industry, or own personal name), Reputation.com (to manage your online and offline reputation), AudienceBloom.com (to improve search engine rankings)

Hiring: Startuply at Crunchbase.com, AngelList.com, StartupHire. Com, Stackoverflow.com, Idealist.org, Craigslist.com

Contact Research: Newsle.com, FullContact.com, Conspire.com, Rapportive.com

Crowdfunding: Kickstarter.com, Indiegogo.com, Microventures.com

LIST OF INTERVIEWED FOUNDERS:

70 founders were interviewed for this book. Below are the founders that are named in the book.

Ann Chao—Sonation

Arabella Simpkin—Greyscale

Bailey Ernstes—MonitorMed Solutions

Ben Jabbawy—Privy.com

Ben Rubin—Change Collective

Chase Garbarino—BostonInno

Chibueze Ihenacho—ARMR Systems

Desmond Lim—Quikforce

Elad Shoushan—LTG Exam Prep Platform

Florence Dennis—African Snack Company

Frank Yao—Smith Street Solutions

Homan Yuen—Solar Junction

Jamie Beaton—Crimson Consulting

Jerrit Tan—Canopy Apps

Joseph Walish—Thermeleon

Joshua Redstone—Equatine Labs

Ken Fan—Ad Gene

Kyle Kahveci—Advanced Continuing Education Association

Lindsay Hyde—Strong Girls, Strong Women

Lisa Walker—LearningInSync

Liz Kwo—New Pathways Education and Technology Group

Manik Suri—MeWe

Mee-Jung Jang—Voncierge

Michael Lisovetsky—Homeswipe

Michael Schmidt—Vaska Technologies

Michele Lunati—Potluck Energy

Nick Dougherty—VerbalCare

Olga Kotsur—Mercaux

Omar Abudayyeh—Modalyst

Rayfil Wong—ProfessorSavings

Roger Ying—Pandai.cn

Sara Gragnolati—Cocomama Foods

Senthil Balasubramanian—Sistine Solar

Shantanu Gaur—Allurion Technologies

Stefanie Botelho—Fitzroy Toys

Vienne Cheung—VienneMilano

Zac Aghion—Splitforce

Index

About the Author

Barbara Hou is the former executive co-director for Harvard Innovations and Ventures in Education (HIVE), a campus organization that supports educational entrepreneurship at Harvard University. Previously, she founded the Asian Women's Leadership University (AWLU) Project, a 501(c)(3) educational startup dedicated to establishing a global women's leadership university based in Asia. She has also practiced as a corporate lawyer in the Hong Kong offices of Cleary Gottlieb Steen & Hamilton LLP and Allen & Overy LLP. She is a graduate of Smith College and the University of Michigan Law School.

She is currently completing her doctorate at Harvard University where she studies the ethics of organizational leadership, adult learning theories, and social entrepreneurship. In her free time, she enjoys advising young entrepreneurs, swimming at Walden Pond, running along the Charles River and evening strolls through the back streets of Cambridge. To learn about upcoming talks, go to www.startupsdemystified.com.

www.ingramcontent.com/pod-product-compliance
Lightning Source LLC
Chambersburg PA
CBHW072302210326
41519CB00057B/2546